MW01027122

Spiritual Cleansings
& Psychic Defenses

by Robert Laremy

Original Publications

SPIRITUAL CLEANSINGS
AND PSYCHIC DEFENSES
By Robert Laremy

© ORIGINAL PUBLICATIONS 2001

ISBN: 0-942272-72-2

FIRST EDITION
First Printing 2001

Cover art and interior illustrations by Raul Canizares

Original Publications
P.O. Box 236
Old Bethpage, New York 11804-0236
(516) 454-6809

Printed in the United States of America

TABLE OF CONTENTS

INTRODUCTION

The thought of allowing anyone to invade your physical safety and that of your loved ones will seem preposterous and unacceptable to most people. The great majority of you will admit to the need of having locks in the doors and windows of your homes and businesses to keep away prowlers and burglars. You also take care to place valuables such as money in safe places such as banks. You will also realize the importance of taking care of your bodies and making sure you and your loved ones eat healthy and protect your well-being by ingesting vitamins and nutritious foods. Yet an astounding number of people do not protect themselves and their loved ones adequately against psychic attacks. The excuse most often given for such actions is *"I don't believe in what I don't see."*

Well, up until relatively recent times humankind had not developed the technology to actually *"see"* microbes, bacteria, and viruses. Even today, the majority of people do not see these agents of disease, but they trust the scientists who with the use of microscopes are able to see these diminutive causes of disease, and who are able to devise defenses against them. The pioneers who maintained that certain diseases were caused by microbes, bacteria, and viruses once stood outside empirical science, yet their assertions were eventually proven correct and natural. Psychic attacks and spiritual maladies today stand outside the realm of empirical science, and the men and women who know how to combat them are not considered to be fighting natural causes. Yet, what is hocus-pocus today may prove to be factual tomorrow once a method of observation is devised, the equivalent of a microscope.

That psychic attacks and spiritual maladies are real can be inferred by their effects on their victims. That there are ways of fighting these attacks can be demonstrated by time-honored methods perfected by practitioners and pioneers who have dedicated their lives to fighting these insidious and pernicious agents of distress. Variously called shamans, gurus, medicine men and women, priests, ceremonial magicians, curanderos, paleros, and santeros, among many other names, these men and women that for the purposes of clarity and simplicity in this book I'll collectively call "spiritual practitioners" share many common traits. Among these are; respect for the environment; a refusal to limit their vision to that which is palpable and material; a willingness to allow the Divine to be expressed through their practices; a life-long dedication to learning their craft from others who have done the same; and an indomitable spirit that has been sorely tested but has emerged victorious in what western ceremonial magicians refer to as "crossing the abyss."

The sources of negative, harmful vibrations are varied. The most common are:

1. People who are not intentionally evil, but who for karmic reasons I can't fully understand are cursed with the "Evil Eye," variously called Malocchio, Mal de Ojo, and Male di Vecchio.

2. People who have intentionally dedicated themselves to the path of evil and are willing and conscious agents of chaos.

3. People who are not consistently evil, but who from time to time may send negativity to people they feel deserve it.

4. Other sources of negative vibrations are places where heinous acts have been committed, causing some of the residual energy created by these acts to become part of the place, like electricity being stored in a battery, and places in the planet, such as some volcanoes in Hawaii, that are charged with so much

power that committing certain taboo acts, such as taking stones from the volcano without permission from the deities that rule there, bring on negativity to the perpetrator.

I experienced the phenomenon of a place that was negatively charged when a Melkite Catholic priest, well known as an exorcist, who is a dear friend asked me to go with him to bless a house one of his parishioners was buying. It was a very large wooden and stone colonial structure in New Jersey, nestled among rolling hills with a lovely brook running through the property. The house had been acquired for a ridiculously low price, allegedly because it was haunted. The minute we walked in, both the priest and I felt an evil, thick, invisible presence, like a wall of cold vapor. A chill went up my spine and my hairs stood on end. My friend looked at me and said, "Oh oh!"' He wore his stole and took holy water out of his bag, but before he could start the blessing, a strange metal instrument resembling pliers flew across the room, almost hitting him on the head! I then began to perceive a noise, muffled but clearly audible, coming out of the wooden floors. It sounded like a chorus of wailing children. I asked my friend if he heard something strange, he nodded yes. After reading a prayer from his book and splashing holy water all around, the vibratory frequency of the room no longer felt charged with negativity, but he told me that he did not feel like the house had been truly freed, that he would have to return again and perhaps do a full rite of exorcism.

By this time, discreetly, as not to offend my friend, whose religion did not allow him to communicate with the dead, I invoked my spirit guide, who told me that the place had been an abortion mill in the 19th century, and the instrument that had been hurled at the priest was used in taking fetuses out of women. Later on my friend investigated the house and found that this had been the case. It took the priest three sessions to spiritually cleanse the place.

Finally, another cause of negativity is karmic consequences for our own actions. The best remedy for this is to avoid acts that may cause the accumulation of bad karma, that is, live a life dedicated to seeking the Light, trying to access your higher self, and doing your best to be a source of goodness and harmony.

The techniques and practices described in this book are meant for everyone. No special training or supernatural power is needed to successfully employ the cleansings described here. Most of the books dealing with psychic self-defense, including Dion Fortune's classic *"Psychic Self Defense"* [1] and Aleister Crowley's monumental *"Magick in Theory and Practice"* appear to be geared towards the ceremonial magician and, ideally, should be read under the guidance of an experienced teacher. In India, the method of passing not only knowledge, but "supernatural" power *(shakti)* from teacher to student is called *Parampara,* the actual transmission of the power is called *shaktipad.* In certain Christian churches the mystical transmission of Christ's charisma to practitioners usually called bishops is called *"apostolic succession,"* usually passed-on through the laying-on of hands. The Roman Catholic Church, Eastern Orthodox churches, and the Church of England can trace their lineage all the way back to Christ and St. Peter 2000 years ago. It usually takes three bishops to consecrate a new one. The Mormon church, which actually pays more attention to the psychic defense of its members than most other Christian churches, believes that John the Baptist, Jesus, and God himself anointed Joseph Smith directly in 1830, empowering him to start a new line of apostolic succession not depending on the Catholic lineage. The Mormons have trained personnel called patriarchs, elders, seventies, and even twelve apostles presided by a prophet, as well as special temples not open to everyone, all dedicated to the spiritual health of their members. Native Americans also possess knowledge of how to deflect psychic attacks through the use of specific rituals. Anyone interested in becoming a spiritual practitioner should seek out a teacher and begin to study in earnest, but for the rest of you, I recommend that you follow the instructions given in this book without the slightest deviation.

All of the procedures described in this book are safe and effective. I have tried most of them personally in thirty-eight years as a spiritual practitioner. The few I have not tried myself have been tried and tested true by friends, teachers, and members of my family. They will work for anyone, regardless of their experience, as long as the procedures are followed to a *"t,"* without any deviation, experimentation, or substitutions. I recommend that you use the information wisely, to help yourself and your loved ones.

Do not presume to be a spiritual practitioner just because you've read this book, trying to heal others outside your immediate circle. I received initiation thirty-eight years ago and have continued to study continually since then, yet I still have a long way to go before I could presume to call myself an absolute master on the subject. Psychic attacks are real and debilitating. Negative vibrations can be as harmful as bacteria, germs, and viruses. This book is intended as an over-the-counter prescription to be used by anyone being victimized by these agents of chaos.

Chapter 1
PREPARATIONS

I - PREPARING YOUR SPACE

One of the most insidious effects of psychic attacks is that it robs its victim of vitality and clear thinking. The victim of a spiritual malaise will often find himself or herself tired, confused, unable to make even the most simple decisions. In fact, when a normally energetic person begins to show signs of mental sluggishness, even experiencing difficulty deciding such simple tasks as what to cook for dinner, this is a good indicator that such a person is being psychically attacked. When a person is being psychically attacked, he will often experience a state of generalized anxiety, an unnerving discomfort the source of which he won't be able to pin-point. One of the first tell-tale signs of psychic attacks is a dull, relentless, headache, usually localized in one particular quarter of the brain. A person who is experiencing discomfort due to spiritual interference will have been a victim of one or more of the following:

■ THE "EVIL EYE."

■ PSYCHIC ATTACK from a practitioner of evil magic. The actual "weapon" the magician will have used includes demons, tormented souls, elementals, and, perhaps the most pernicious, your own state of mind manipulated by a superior evil force.

- Psychic attack from an ENERGY VAMPIRE.
- Negativity picked up at a "haunted" place.
- Unwanted communications from the dead.

I will treat each of these subjects separately in the following pages. Now let us go over some preliminary steps that will go a long way towards preparing you to be healed of the spiritual malady that ails you. These include preparing your space to receive positive vibrations,, as well as preparing yourself through the act of performing a simple meditation. Firstly, you must use the following psychic cleansers, Cascarilla and Florida Water, in the manner prescribed.

CASCARILLA. Cascarilla is a spiritual cleansing agent developed by African-Cuban practitioners. It resembles a little white chalky bonbon and is available in every botanica. It is the spiritual cleanser of choice employed in the Santeria and Spiritism religions of Latin America.[2] Practitioners developed cascarilla as a replacement for pembe, a ritual white or yellow chalk still employed by African and South American practitioners of Nganga, Candomble, and other religions having roots in West Africa. Cascarilla is powerful because it is made out of dried, powdered eggshells. The egg is a powerful symbol of potentiality. It is life in a capsule. Nutritionally speaking, it is the perfect food for humans, the best source of protein. We'll have more on eggs in a later chapter.

The way to use cascarilla is simple, just draw crosses with it behind doors, on top of windows, by your bed, by the crib of a baby, and inside your vehicle. Drawing cascarilla crosses on your forhead, temples, hands, and the soles of your feet temporarily frees you from the effects of psychic attacks, allowing you to think clearly and strongly so you may enact more durable solutions. Cascarilla acts as a repellant of negative vibrations. It also keeps away the spirits of the dead. If you have a positive relationship with a spirit of a person who passed on, as opposed to a spirit of an angel or other non-human intelligence, then do not put cascarilla on your person, for it is my experience that the vibratory frequence of cascarilla makes it difficult for the dead to communicate with the living, regardless of whether the dead are good or evil.

FLORIDA WATER. A usual companion of cascarilla is a cologne-like substance called "Florida Water." Florida Water is one of the most commonly employed spiritual cleansers commercially available, yet how it came to occupy such an important place in the arsenal of many spiritual practitioners is a story worth telling.

In the late 19th century, a New York company called Murray and Lanman came up with an after shave called Florida Water that had a sweet, piquant smell. It contained such spices as cinnamon and orange blossom, and was alcohol based. The fragrance did not become popular as an after shave, but in the meantime Cuban practitioners noticed that when they wore the after shave it was as if the gates to the beyond had busted open! Communications with the dead that would require hours to accomplish would take only minutes when they were wearing the after shave. It didn't take long for them to realize that it was the Florida Water that was making the difference. Furthermore, the spirits that were being attracted by the essence were only those of high vibratory frequency! Without realizing it, Murray and Lanman had come up with a perfect psychic emollient, a unique blend of flowers, spices, and alcohol that couldn't have been more appropriate to the spiritual practices of the people who adopted Florida Water as their basic psychic cleanser and facilitator of communications with spirit guides.

Because cascarilla repels bad spirits and Florida Water attracts good spirits, they form a perfect combination.

In preparing your space to receive spiritual healing, freely splash Florida Water all around. Florida Water today is almost exclusively used for spiritual purposes. It is available in all botanicas as well as numerous drug stores and bodegas wherever Spanish-speaking Caribbean people reside.[3] Now that you have prepared your space to receive high vibrations, you may prepare yourself with the following simple, yet powerful meditation.

INCENSE AND SAGE. After using cascarilla and Florida Water, use some incense or sage to complete the preparation of your space. The best clearing incenses are Benzoin and Three Kings, which is usually a mixture of Myhrr, Frankincense, and Benzoin. Dragon's Blood incense is also an excellent dissipator of negativity. Burn only natural, high quality products. Stay away from cheap sticks ("pumps") that contain sawdust and, sometimes, lard, which is then dipped in chemicals. Use only handrolled Indian masala sticks, such as Satya Sai Baba brand Nag Champa incense, or better yet, use gum incense that is burned on a charcoal. Use self-igniting charcoal, available in stores that sell religious articles - Botanicas, Incense and Oil stores, and at outside stands where vendors sell incense. Make sure to place burning charcoal on a safe surface, such as a cast iron incense burner. Do not place hot charcoal on a porcelain or china dish, for the heat will cause the dish to crack. An empty can of tuna fish, upside-down on a dish, can serve as a make-shift holder for a hot charcoal. Before adding incense to charcoal, you must wait for the rim of the lighted charcoal to turn grey, then add a little incense at a time.

Dried sage tied into a six-inch, cigar-like bundle, called a "smudge," makes an excellent clearing incense when lighted. The best incense for relaxing, however, is Nag Champa.

RUM AND CIGAR SMOKE. While rum and tobacco have a somewhat problematic connotation in America because people abuse them as substances, in South America and the Caribbean spiritual practitioners have used them, especially tobacco, for hundreds of years as excellent clearing agents. The best way to clear a space with rum is to get some in your mouth and spray it out as a fine mist. The technique for doing this takes some practice; it involves pursing your lips tightly, filling your mouth with air until your cheeks puff up, and then forcing the rum out by rapidly blowing it out creating a fine mist. Working with the cigar also involves some practice, for you must put the lit end inside your mouth, blowing the smoke out through the part that normally goes inside your mouth. BE VERY CAREFUL NOT TO BURN YOURSELF!

II-PREPARATORY MEDITATION

It would be unrealistic to expect a person being victimized by any form of spiritual interference to have the presence of mind to engage in long, complicated forms of meditation. Some simple techniques, however, have been proven effective in preparing the way for spiritual cleansings. The state of tranquil peace and contentment achieved with the aid of the technique I'm about to describe is antithetical to the state of chaotic confusion and despair caused by psychic attacks, thus the performance of the following meditation will help you achieve success in more quickly ridding yourself of the unwanted spiritual malaise.

CHOOSING YOUR SPACE. Before engaging in any form of meditation, there are some simple steps you must take to make sure your environment is conducive to achieving the peaceful state you seek. The first thing you must do is choose a place where you wont be disturbed. This could be your bedroom, but I recommend you use a recliner rather than lay on a bed during the exercise, since a bed could make you too comfortable and you may fall asleep prematurely--it's OK to drift to a peaceful sleep *after* completing excercise. After choosing the place, clean it and place everything in order. Dirt and disorder are the enemies of peace and tranquility. Light a purple candle and a stick of Nag Champa incense before setting down to meditate, and read the 23rd Psalm with a sincere heart. Before you settle down to meditate, however, take care to engage your hearing in either listening to peaceful, unobstrusive music, preferably instrumental, or by providing yourself with white noise, such as that produced by a fan, a window air conditioner, or a CD of ocean sounds, forest sounds etc.

PREPARING YOURSELF. Sit or lay back, gently close your eyes, and place your arms limply by your sides, letting them rest on the armrests of the recliner, palms open facing upward. Beginning from the top of your head, visualize all of your muscles relaxing. Imagine a soft, purple light entering your head, filling your head, making each muscle in your face relax, each muscle on your neck relax, then feel the relaxing light enter the nape of your neck relaxing it, then the shoulder muscles, the muscles on your back; feel the relaxing purple light spill over both arms, relaxing your biceps,, your triceps, and continuing down your forearms to your hands, to the tip of your fingers. Feel the relaxing purple light sweep down from your neck relaxing your chest muscles, your abdomen, your lower back, your buttocks, your groin, and down your thighs, you feel the warm, comforting purple light relax your legs, down to your feet, and to your toes. Your entire body is now thoroughly relaxed. You will now clearly state in your mind the following:

"I will take ten deep breaths, at the end of which I will be in a state of total relaxation, allowing goodness and positivity to enter my life."

Proceed to slowly take ten deep breaths. Be aware of each breath, visualize the air entering your nostrils, slowly filling your lungs with life-giving oxygen. Retain the air in your body for a second, then slowly exhale it through your mouth, allowing negativity and stress to leave your body with each exhalation. After the tenth breath, imagine a peaceful beach, or a rolling green hill, or even a blank movie screen, whatever gives you a sense of peace. If outside worries try to interfere with your meditation, do not fight them. Let them go through and just think of yourself as detached from them, as if you were a spectator rather than an actor in such a drama. Once you feel a special kind of tranquility, where your thoughts no longer race and your surroundings disappear, you are ready to say your mantra, the phrase that will prepare you to receive any cleansing.

THE MANTRA. Eastern peoples have long known the power of the word. Buddhism and Hinduism make ample use of repetition of phrases and sounds in order to achieve power. Eastern Christians chant the Jesus prayer on their Jesus beads just as Buddhists chant their mantras on their malas. A seventy-year-old Indian guru named Prabhupada brought the power of the Hare Krishna mantra to the West in the 1960s. He arrived in America with less than ten dollars in his pocket. By 1970 he headed a multi-national movement worth millions of dollars, all built on the power of the simple mantra *"Hare Krishna Hare Krishna Krishna Krishna Hare Hare Hare Rama Hare Rama Rama Rama Hare Hare."*

The mantra that accompanies the meditation I am describing here is in English, yet when done as described, it is as powerful as any exotic Sanskrit or Tibetan phrase. When you are ready, begin to utter the phrase, *"Peace, Be Still, and Know That I Am God"* over and over. First say the phrase in your head, then softly mutter it, slowly raising the volume of your voice with each utterance until you've achieved a comfortable volume, one that resonates with your soul. After about fifteen minutes of doing this *(just calculate it in your mind, it doesn't have to be exact)* stop saying the phrase. Thank the Universe for what you have experienced. Finally, visualize the purple light of relaxation leaving your body in exactly the opposite way it entered, until it leaves the crown of your head, leaving you feeling relaxed, fortified, and whole, and ready to tackle any psychic malaise.

Chapter 2
DEFENSE AGAINST
THE EVIL EYE

I-WHAT THE EVIL EYE IS

When I was a child and my little brother an infant, I remember a horrified woman approaching my mother and telling her that she had inarvetedly cast the evil eye on my little brother by saying to herself, *"What a lovely child!"* She proceeded to lightly spank the baby, having; everyone say *"God bless him,"* and telling my mother that whenever anyone would praise the baby, she should think the phrase *"besale el culito."* My mother was a spiritual practitioner who had a scientist's love of research. As unbelievable as it seems, she befriended the woman in order to more fully understand the causes and effects of the Evil Eye, taking on the challenge of perhaps "curing" the woman, called La Hondureña. La Hondureña claimed that her mother's mother had cursed her, condemming her own daughter to give birth to a carrier of the Evil Eye. La Hondureña said all her life she had been a pariah, being thrown out of every place she lived in her native Honduras once her malady was discovered. She said she tried to do good by casting the Evil Eye on people who she thought deserved it. The sad aspect of her plight is that she did not want to have this so-called power, and she felt herself a victim of it. But, what exactly is "the evil eye?"

HISTORICAL PERSPECTIVE. Most cultures have a version of the evil eye. In Italy it is called *"Malocchio" or "Male di Vecchio"*, in Spain and Latin America *"Mal de Ojo"*. Like La Hondurena, many people afflicted with possession of evil eyes were cursed by workers of evil, usually before they were born. A mother can transfer the condition to a child, a husband to a wife. The road that facilitates the aquisition of the evil eye is envy. People who suffer from feeling envy often develop the evil eye. In the Ten Commandments we find an injunction against coveting other people's wives and property. While it is not evil to be inspired by the attainment of others, motivating ourselves to work harder so we can have things like they have, to feel anger and sadness over someone else's good fortune is envy. Envy is truly the proverbial green-eyed monster that destroys both the victim and the perpetrator. I knew a woman in the West Indies who would visit her prosperous sister, sit quitely on a chair in the kitchen, and start to cry about how good her sister had it in comparison with her. Invariably, shortly after this woman's visit, the prosperous one would experience debilitating illnesses, and would suffer economically also.

The Evil Eye is an energy that, in the case of most people, cannot be controlled. It flows out of their eyes without them being able to control it. Sleeping infants are the most vulnerable. Because some people are not aware that they possess the Evil Eye, no one should compliment sleeping infants without saying *"God bless him"* immediately after. Saying "God bless him" interferes with the transference of evil energy.[4] The Bible says, *"If thine eye offend thee, pluck it out."* (Mr. 9:47). There are cases of people actually plucking their eyes out after finding out they possessed this malady.

II-TREATMENT

PREVENTING THE EVIL EYE. In the Spanish-speaking Caribbean the most common and effective method of protecting children from the evil eye is to pin an Azabache bead to their shirt, or having them wear one on a gold chain around the neck. Azabache is Spanish for jet, a hard, black variety of lignite which takes a high polish and is used in jewelry as if it were a semi-precious stone, even though jet comes from trees. For maximum protection, the bead, about the size of a small green pea, is joined to an even smaller bead of red coral, another substance known for its protective qualities. The traditional way the Azabache is shaped is either as a faceted round bead or smoothed out like a marble. At present it is common to see Azabaches in the shape of little hands making a fist, the thumb portruding from between the index and third fingers. Or, in the shape of a hand making the sign of the "Devil's horns." The simple round bead is most effective. Wash the bead in either holy water or ocean water before using.

In Europe, garlic, vervain, and wolfbane are used to avert the Evil Eye. Wearing religious symbols with devotion and respect also keep the Evil Eye away, but these only work for sincere believers. If you wear a Cross simply because it is fashionable, it won't work.

While the following preventive method may disgust certain individuals, urine baths have been used as spiritual cleansers in Africa and the Middle East for ages. Put a couple of drops of urine caught midstream when you wake up in the morning in your bathwater and your floor wash and you'll prevent the Evil Eye. Some people substitute beer for urine, but it is not quite as effective.

GETTING RID OF THE EVIL EYE. While the charms and simple techniques discussed above will serve to avert the influx of the Evil Eye, once its baneful effects have penetrated your soundness, you must take more drastic steps to get rid of it. The following procedure is relatively easy to do and has been successfully employed for hundreds of years.

STEP 1   Relax or meditate on becoming whole again. (*see chapter 1*).

STEP 2   Light a black figure candle, dressed with Magnet oil, and place it near bathtub.

STEP 3   Fill tub with warm water and add three bay leaves, a sprig of rosemary, and some sea salt to the water.

STEP 4   Relax in the tub for twenty minutes, make sure you can observe the lighted black candle. Will your malady to be transferred to the candle, and visualize it being burned away.

STEP 5   Come out of bathtub and pass an egg all over your body, make sure you do not miss any part of your body.

STEP 6   Take remains of candle, remains of the bath, and egg, place on a paper bag. Pat dry yourself and dress to go outside.

STEP 7   Throw bag with contents over fence of a cemetery, do not look back. Keep on walking and go home a different route you used to get to the cemetery. You are now free of the deleterious effects of the evil eye. In the future, make use of preventive measures to avoid being victimized again.

CAN RELIGION CLEAR YOU OF THE EVIL EYE? Some people really do find freedom from this malady by joining a fundamentalist religion. These religions, including--but not limited to-so-called born-again Christianity, rely on surrendering your soul to a savior figure who then takes on your karma, freeing you from spiritual maladies. While it is true that joining groups such as the Jehovah's Witnesses, Pentecostals, and Hare Krishnas may free you from the Evil Eye, you also give up a lot by joining them.

Mainly, you give up your individuality, your right to question God, and the right to be responsible for your own actions. While you may find it odd to see Jehovah's Witnesses and Hare Krishnas mentioned in the same breath, they are more alike than you may realize. Both religions exhibit traits of devotional religiosity, which Hindus call "bhakti, " which is Sanskrit for "devotion." Taking this action (joining a fundamentalist church) would only give you results if your character ("temperament") is what the Hindus call "tamasic. " Therefore, if you are considering joining a religious group to free yourself from psychic attack, you should first determine if your temperament is tamasic. In fact, it may be of some help to you to find out where you fit in the Hindu schema. Practitioners in the ancient Indian art of Ayurveda prescribe herbal remedies based on the patient's temperament according to an age-old manner of classification which we give you here, in a much-abridged form.

Hinduism teaches that there are different types of religious expressions suited to different types of people, no religion being intrinsically superior to the other. The three main types of people are characterized by temperaments, called "gunas." These gunas are *sattva* (purity, clarity), *rajas* (passion), and *tamas* (inertia). The religious expressions, or spiritualities, are: *Jnana, karma, and bhakti.*

Jnana is the path of intelligence, discrimination (in the positive sense of the word), and mental and spiritual growth. It views God as no different from one's Higher Self. Jnana is the path of sattvic people. Ralph Waldo Emerson, Krishnamurti, and Howard Thurman taught different versions of the path of sattva.

Karma is the path of good deeds, the way of redemption through social change. Karma is the path of Rajasic people. It seeks to serve God through active service to other humans, prioritizing spiritual well-being over physical comfort. Mahatma Ghandi, Martin Luther King, and Albert Schweizer each exemplify the path of karma.

Tamas is the path of least resistance, you give your burden to Jesus, you trust that by continually repeating the name of Krishna in Hinduism or the 99 attributes of Allah in Islam, you will attain liberation not through your own merits, but due to someone else's merit. Nichiren, Billy Graham, and Bhaktivedanta Swami Prabhupada exemplify the path of tamas. Based on the descriptions given above, you may intuit whether you are a sattvic, rajasic, or tamasic person. Following are some procedures appropriate to each of the three gunas.

SATTVIC RESPONSE TO THE EVIL EYE. Meditate according to the formula discussed in Chapter One, except that after repeating the mantra *"Peace, Be Still, And Know That I Am God"* for approximately ten times, you should switch to the universal mantra, *"Aum."* Since Aum contains the vibratory frequencies of creation, by chanting it over and over you will create an environment antithetical to the Evil Eye, which thrives on frequencies of destruction. As the energy that we call "Evil Eye" begins to lose strength in face of the stronger power of the AUM mantra, the sattvic person will visualize all the evil eye energy coming together in the spot of his body where it had caused the most physical discomfort. Let's say the left temple, where a consistent, dull, headache had been bothering you for example. Imagine the evil eye coming together to form a small, black ball, then visualize all the power within you that is identical to God's saving energy forming a blueish-purplehand that grabs the insignificant little ball of negativity you had gathered, throwing it far away from you! Visualize the hand actually hurling the ball with incredible strength, so far away from you it will never be able to return again. Repeat this operation three nights in a row to make sure this particular attack of Evil Eye has been erradicated. To prevent further attacks, the sattvic person develops a regimen of daily meditation and visualization, always striving to uncover his true divine nature.

RAJASIC RESPONSE TO THE EVIL EYE. If you are action oriented, a doer, a person who derives pleasure from causing positive changes in his physical milieu, you are a rajasic person. Because people of a rajasik nature are always "out there" among fellow humans, constantly performing god deeds, they tend to be more exposed to the sight of people who have the Evil Eye. For this reason, rajasik people need to pay special attention to preventive measures. Once afflicted, however, the rajasik person needs to take active steps to erradicate his condition.

STEP 1   Go to seven different Catholic, Eastern Ortrhodox, or High Episcopalian churches (any one denomination or combination of any of these listed will do) within a space of seven days, and collect holy water from each after having left a donation in the poor box of each of at least one dollar.

STEP 2   After adding the holy water to your bathwater (keeping a little for later use), arrange to have three people you have helped in the past read the prayer to Saint Louis Bertrand (San Luis Beltran) to you while you are lying down. Each person must read it through once, using a leaf of fresh basil cut and made in the form of a cross to bless you with. This is done by dipping the basil leaf cross in the seven-holy-waters mixture each time this sign appears, ✠, and symbolically doing the sign of the cross over you. After the first person performs the prayer, he or she must leave your presence without seeing, or even knowing, who the other two people reading the prayer for you are--in fact, each of the three readers must not know who else is reading the prayer for you. All three must read the prayer within a twenty-four hour period. After the third person has blessed you with St. Louis's prayer, you will be rid of the effects of the evil eye. Here is the prayer:

PRAYER OF SAINT LOUIS BELTRAN
*This prayer has been used to ward off the evil eye
for hundreds of years.*

Creature of God, I exorcize, treat, and bless you
in the name of the Holy Trinity.

Father ✞, Son ✞, and Holy Spirit ✞, Three different persons and one true essence; and of the Virgin Mary, Our Lady, conceived without stain of original sin. Virgin before giving birth ✞, during birth ✞, and after the birth ✞, by the glorious St. Gertrude, your beloved and given spouse, by the Eleven Thousand Virgins, by Saint Joseph, Saint Rocco, and Saint Sebastian, and by all the saints of your celestial court, by your Very Glorious Incarnation ✞, Very Glorious Birth ✞, Very Holy Passion ✞, Very Glorious Resurrection ✞, and Divine Ascencion ✞. By so high and holy mysteries that I in truth believe, I plead to your Divine Majesty, placing as intercessessor your Divine Mother, Our Advocate, that you liberate and heal this afflicted creature of any sickness, evil eye, pain, accident, or fever, or any any other injury, wound, or malady, Amen Jesus.

Not looking at the unworthy person ✞ who would prefer such sacrosanct mysteries, with such good faith I plead to you, oh Lord, for your greater glory and devotion of those present, that you will by your piety and mercy heal or liberate from this wound, affliction, pain, humor, sickness, taking it away from this part and place. And may your Divine Majesty not allow accident, corruption, or injury to overcome him,[5] giving him health so that, with it, he may serve you and fulfill your Most Holy Will. ✞ Amen Jesus.

I exorcize and treat you, and Jesus Christ Our Lord heals you, blesses you, and lets unfold his Divine Will. Amen Jesus. Consumatum est ✞, Consumatum est ✞, Consumatum est ✞ [6]

TAMASIC RESPONSE TO THE EVIL EYE. If your temperament is one of devotion to God in the form of adoration of his image and surrender of your self, if you feel that prayer is the strongest medicine, you are tamasic in character. The following treatment for the evil eye will help you get rid of its noxious effects.

STEP 1   With a devoted heart, pray to God to help you erradicate the evil eye. If you are a Christian, pray the Lord's Prayer. If you believe at all in the Bible, pray the 23rd Psalm and the 100th Psalm with fervor each night by the light of a purple candle.

STEP 2   Put a clear glass of water under your bed before going to sleep, ask in your prayer that all negativity, evil, bad thoughts, evil eye, and bad vibrations go into that glass of water. In the morning, upon waking up, flush the water down the toilet while saying *"May all negativity, evil eye, and maleficent energy be flushed away with this water."*

STEP 3   After seven days of performing steps one and two, make an amulet as follows: Write line five of the 100th Psalm on a parchment--in ancient times it was done using one's own blood--then fold and fold again until a tiny size is reached. At this point, seal with black wax from a candle. Keep adding wax to the neatly folded parchment until it is completely covered, then tie enough string around wax-covered parchment until it has the appearance of a ball. Cover ball completely with more black wax. The resulting amulet is one of the most potent protective devices known. Keep in a safe place, or carry with you for extra protection.

AMULETS AGAINST THE EVIL EYE. There are many amulets to ward off the evil eye, most of them work better if you believe in them. Religious symbols such as crosses, Stars of David, medals depicting saints, rosaries, and Buddhist and Hindu malas that have been properly blessed are efficacious only as long as you believe in their power and the power of the religion each represents. The following objects carry protection on their own, regardless of whether you believe or not: Jet, red coral, wood from the silk cotton tree, garlic, wolfbane, laurel, camphor, mothballs, and vervain. Many people in Cuba keep a drawing of an eye under which a slightly open mouth reveals a protruding tongue with a knife going through it, as a talisman to avoid being the object of envy, wagging tongues, and the evil eye.

Chapter 3
DEFENSE AGAINST PSYCHIC ATTACK
FROM PRACTITIONERS OF EVIL MAGIC

I-IDENTIFYING THE PRACTITIONER OF EVIL MAGIC

WHAT IS A PRACTITIONER OF EVIL MAGICK? [7] Some individuals choose to align themselves with the powers of the left-hand side, the destructive aspects of existence. Either by ignorance, avarice, pain, or simply free will, some people choose to do harm to others, some making doing harm a way of life. These practitioners are variously known as black magicians, evil sorcerers, macumbeiros and mayomberos.[8] Also, some practitioners such as ceremonial magicians, wizards, warlocks, santeros, paleros, witches, voodoo priests, and medicine men and women, do not limit their practice exclusively to works of good, many also engaging in dark works if they deem it necessary to do so. These people send you bad energy either because they want to for personal reasons, or they do so on behalf of another, such as a client, who has petitioned that bad things are sent to you. Other people who normally don't practice evil magic may do so under special circumstances. Let's say, for example, that you are a man who unilaterally decides to end a relationship that was not working for you, but your partner doesn't agree with you. They say hell hath no fury like a woman scorned. The truth is, any jilted lover, regardless of whether a woman or a man is in question, will feel hurt and, in this state of mind, may engage in acts that under other circumstances they'd never consider, such as sending destructive psychic energy to the one who caused their pain.

II-GENERAL PREVENTIVE MEASURES AGAINST PSYCHIC ATTACKS FROM PRACTITIONERS OF EVIL MAGIC

SANTERIA PROCEDURE TO ENSURE SUCCESS IN SENDING BAD ENERGY BACK

Assuming the practitioner who sent you bad energy knew what he or she was doing, he or she must have taken some steps to guard against the bad energy's return. In most cases, the following procedure weakens most sorcerers' defenses so that their nefarious dispatches can be safely returned to them.

STEP 1   Get a white candle, light it at midnight before performing any work.

STEP 2   Offer a brand new white ceramic or china plate filled with fruit, along with the candle, to the guardian angel of the person you are to address.

STEP 3   Say *"In the name of God, sweet guardian angel of _____ , I COMPELL you to come and see what bountiful fruits and light I offer you. As you partake of this feast, oh sweet angel, I ask you to permit me to teach the person you protect a hard lesson so he (she) will receive a just payback for his action. I call upon Eshu and the Lords of Karma to witness this action. Amen! Amen! Amen!*

SANTERIA SPELL TO SEND BACK A PSYCHIC ATTACK

Ingredients

*A pig's tongue • Red cayenne pepper • Vinegar
21 thin nails • Brown paper bag*

STEP 1   Using a lead pencil; write full name of person who has been sending you bad energy on a brown paper strip cut out of a brown paper grocery bag.

STEP 2   Split the tongue lengthwise, place paper with name on it inside split tongue.

STEP 3   Trap the paper inside split tongue by sealing the tongue with 21 nails.

STEP 4   Sprinkle vinegar and cayenne pepper on tongue, throw in middle of busy highway, where many vehicles will trample on it, at the hour of midday.

SENDING IT BACK WITH PSALMS. Psalms have been used to send back evil energy by practitioners named Kabbalists for hundreds of years. The following are the most potent Psalms used specifically for this purpose, along with the procedure that must be performed in order to reverse a psychic attack. Follow instructions to a *"t"* if you wish to obtain favorable results.

PSALM 83

STEP 1   Scratch the name of the person who is doing evil to you on the side of a black pull-out seven-day candle.

STEP 2   Light candle at midnight on a Thursday.

STEP 3   Read Psalm 83 all the way through each night for seven consecutive nights at the same hour.

Allow candle to burn for seven days or until the candle is totally consumed (if candle does not last for seven days, then light a small black candle each time you need to until all seven readings of the psalm have been done). The evil that had been sent to you will be returned seven-fold to its originator.

PSALM 91

One of the most renowned guards against the Evil Eye and all manner of sortilege, this psalm is attached to babies' clothing to protect them from evil. With a glass of clear water, a white candle, and this psalm, a dwelling can be exorcized of poltergeist activity. No elemental spirit or lesser demon can remain when this psalm is read out loud at the hour of midnight. For best results, there should be three people present, one carrying the glass of water, the other a white candle, while the third reads the psalm in a loud, authoritative voice. This operation shall be carried out three nights in a row. A Bible left open at this psalm will prevent bothersome spirits from returning.

PSALM 118

This psalm is especially useful in eliminating demons. Sit in a tub of warm water to which myrrh, frankincense, and camphor oils have been added. Read the entire psalm seven times while in the water, this should repel any demonic forces that had been around you.

PSALM 129

STEP 1   Write name of whoever or whatever is oppressing you on a sheet of parchment.

STEP 2   Place a glassencased blue candle on top of writing.

STEP 3   Light the candle and pray Psalm 129 each night with fervor and faith, by the time candle is consumed, your oppression will be lifted.

PSALM 139

A very effective Psalm for stopping psychic attacks. Read psalm 139 while holding a glass of water right before you go to sleep, leave glass under your bed, or by your side if you sleep close to the floor, then throw out water to the street when you wake up while saying *"may all manner of evil be thrown out along with this water."*

PSALM 142

For clarity of mind, read this psalm when feelings of confusion and melancholy assault you. After reading Psalm, say *"David this psalm did pray as he pondered in a cave, I do so hope and pray that my Lord my mind will save."*

SENDING IT BACK WITH A CANDLE

If you know who is responsible for your psychic malady, follow the following procedure:

STEP 1 Get a black, seven-day pull-out candle and dress it in Patchouli oil.

STEP 2 Scratch the name of the person on the side of the candle.

STEP 3 During the waning moon, at the hour of midnight, say *"Just Judge, I'm justified!"* Turn the candle upside down and light the candle from the bottom, Say:

"May _____ receive seven-fold what he is sending to me, in the Holy Name of Adonai I ask that this be done!"

(continued)

STEP 4   Do this for three consecutive nights then allow candle to burn through and throw remains over gates of a cemetery.

SENDING IT BACK WITH AN EGG

STEP 1   Paint an egg black, let it stay in your room for nine days.

STEP 2   On the ninth day, pass the egg all over your body, wishing that your psychic malady be transferred to the egg.

STEP 3   If you know who is sending you the negative energy, break the egg as near to their place of residence as possible, if you do not know who is doing this to you, break the egg on a cemetery.

III - MAKING YOUR HOME PSYCHIC-ATTACK PROOF

PROTECTION WITH INCENSE. Although the best way to fumigate a house with incense is to use gum incense burned on self-igniting charcoal, Indian masala insense sticks are also good. Always use natural incenses, avoid artificial scents such as "baby powder", or name brands such as "Polo" or other popular perfume brands. As we have said before, Sage, Frankincense, and Three Kings are the best substances to burn daily in order to stave off the onslaught of psychic attacks. I'll name some of the most popular incenses and their qualities, plus some household spices that can be burned on a charcoal the same as incense.

ABRAMELIN - This incense is made by mixing myrrh, cinnamon, olive oil, and galangal. To be used only by professionals, do not use on your own, unless directed by one who knows.

AMBER - A sweet-smelling incense that attracts sensual goddesses such as Aphrodite and Oshun, burn right before making love. Mixed with a little brown sugar, it leads to close relationships developing among potential lovers who smell it at the same time.

BENZOIN - Usually mixed with frankincense in Greek Orthodox churches, its aroma has the ability to attract angelic forces and high vibrations.

FRANKINCENSE - Mentioned several times in the Bible, this is the spiritual cleansing par excellence when it comes to incenses. It is the "churchie" incense. Burn it in Sundays to attract angelic forces.

MYRRH - So precious that the Wise Men gave the infant Jesus a chest full of it as a gift, myrrh is mixed with frankincense and benzoin to form "three kings incense." Myrrh opens up the astral gates that make it easier for angelic beings to come to our plane. For this reason, it is very useful to burn myrrh along with frankincense, for frankincense attracts the angels, while myrrh facilitates their descent into our world.

NAG CHAMPA - This exquisite Indian incense has been popularized by the Hare Krishna movement. It has a calming effect and tends to uplift the spirits of those who smell its aroma.

SANDALWOOD - Calms the mind, making it receptive to higher spiritual vibrations.

HOUSEHOLD INCENSES
Some spices found in your kitchen serve as incenses
when burned on charcoal.

ALLSPICE - Promotes commerce and positive interactions. Burn at social gatherings.

BAY - Also called laurel. A bay tree keeps away evil spirits. Burning a dry bay leaf on a charcoal keeps away nepharias influences.

CIGARS - Smoke keeps away evil spirits, permitting only good ones to stay.

CINNAMON - Has a sweet, loving fragrance. Burn with a drop of honey to attract love and harmony to your home.

COFFEE - Fresh grounds can be burnt on charcoal to offer protection from nightmares and those who attack while you sleep.

GARLIC PEELINGS - Burned on charcoal, they help clear the troubled mind.

HONEY - A few drops in your charcoal sweetens rhe atmosphere.

ROSEMARY - Burn it to ward off diseases brought about by magic. In a bath, it brings money.

SLOW COOKERS AND POTPOURRIS

Some people who suffer from respiratory illnesses will not tolerate incense smoke. A good alternative is to prepare similar recipes using essential oils as well as dried and/or fresh herbs, nuts, and flowers in a slow cooker, letting a softer kind of smoke (vapor) permeate your space. An excellent repellent of negative energies can be prepared by adding the following ingredients to water being heated in a slow cooker:

1 Bay Leaf • 5 sticks of Cinnamon
• a large Lemon wedge • some Myrrh oil • Sea Salt

PROTECTION WITH WATER. Water is the holiest, most effective, most undervalued psychic cleanser available. Water gathered at different spots under different circumstances have different qualities and powers.

OCEAN WATER. Ocean water is the substance from where creation sprang, one of the most powerful removers of negativity known to man. Sea water gathered at noon on June 24th is particularly powerful, a few drops sprinkled between your sheets protects your psyche while you are asleep, a few drops sprinkled throughout your house prevents evil from entering your abode. Adding sea water to your bath removes effects of the evil eye, psychic attacks, and generalized negativity. Sea water should be collected from an in-coming tide. It is wise to leave a monetary offering as you remove the water. Seven pennies is an acceptable amount. Mopping the floors and sponging the walls of your home with water that has been mixed with sea water further protects your home from psychic attacks.

RIVER WATER. Rivers are the veins that allow the earth's blood (its waters) to flow. River water, as the source of 90% of the world's drinking water, are symbolic of life. Tap water, which is usually nothing more than processed river water, can usualy be substituted for it if river water is not readily available. Intention, incantation, and prayer are what makes tap water the carrier of power. Some particular rivers, such as the Ganges in India, are intrinsically holy. The river Ganges is a manifestation of an Indian goddess, Mata Ganga. The river Jordan is widely believed to possess healing qualities because Jesus was baptized there.

LAKE WATER. I do not recommend using lake water for the removal of negativity, because lakes possess very stable energy. Lake water should be used in works involving stability and permanence, especially regarding an existing relationship.

RAIN WATER. Rain water is used in many Santeria works. It is called "the seed of Shango" and can be drunk by women wanting to become pregnant. The silk cotton tree (ceiba pentandra), also called the Kapok tree by Native Americans, is extremely holy. In the Santeria tradition it is said that rain water which falls into the crevices of this great tree during the month of May is the most powerful spiritual cleanser available. It should be collected and stored in glass containers. The first rain in May is also considered naturally holy.

HOLY WATER. Holy water is common tap water--or any other kind of water--which has been blessed by one or, more commonly, more than one priest in the Catholic, Eastern Orthodox, or High Episcopalian (Anglo-Catholic) churches. Properly, only priesthood holders should consecrate water, but if it is needed in an emergency and no priest is available, a sincere believer may consecrate the water. What follows is the Orthodox prayer of consecration of water.

O Lord, our holy God, who created the universe from
nothing and imposed limits upon the waters by the wisdom
of your power, bless ✠ [9] this water and sanctify it by the
power, action, and descent of your all-holy,
good and life-giving Spirit.
May it bring protection for your servants
from all harm, from the destruction of evil, and freedom
from superstition. May it bring healing for the sick. Make
it a redemption of sins, a cure for the suffering, a
purification of soul and holy and sanctification of homes.
And may it bring healing for the general welfare of all.
Grant sanctification, blessing, and health to all those who
receive it and make use of it. For through this, your name
will be glorified, in the name of
the Father ✠, the Son ✠, and the Holy Spirit ✠,
now and forever and ever, Amen.

While sprinkling holy water around the home, the priest says:

"May this house be blessed ✠ in the name of the Father,
and of the Son, and of the Holy Spirit, Amen."

SPRING WATER. There are several well-known springs that were magically produced. The most famous is at Lourdes, France, the waters of the spring there having healed many people - 63 according to the very stringent tests the Roman Catholic Church applies to each alleged cure. All spring water is conducive to introspection, depth of emotions, and connectedness to your higher self. Since spring water is available in most supermarkets, no one should do without it. Drink it and add it to your bath to promote psychic development. Well water has a similar vibration, but is less proactive, than spring water. Both have masculine vibrations, as they penetrate the earth.

Chapter 4
PROTECTING YOURSELF FROM AN ENERGY VAMPIRE

I—IDENTIFYING THE ENERGY VAMPIRE

WHAT IS AN ENERGY VAMPIRE? Unlike the practitioner of evil magic, the energy vampire doesn't have to perform any ritual in order to cause harm. He or she is a weak individual, a psychic parasite who depends on the energy of stronger individuals for his or her very life! A person may have become an energy vampire because, after consistently spending energy on deleterious pursuits, he or she has been punished by the Universe. Perhaps the energy vampire, like all other parasites, was simply born that way, a karmic consequence of his or her past-life behavior. Whatever the reason for the energy vampire's existence, his/her attacks may prove especially insidious, since he or she may appear to be a pathetic, dependent individual whose need for you may appeal to your sense of generosity. Once you identify the energy vampire, you need to stay as far away from that person as possible.

We have all known people whose very presence seem to drain us of our energy. The sad, lonely co-worker who is forever complaining of how cruel the world is to them, the relative who claims to be victimized by everybody else in the family, the so-called friend who after talking your ear off on the phone tells you how much better she feels, yet you feel depleted for many hours after your talk. Energy vampires are particularly effective in their attacks at night while your defenses are down. For this reason, developing a daily ritual of preemptive defensive actions is important. Sometimes purposefully altering your sleeping pattern confuses the energy vampire. For example, if you are known to work at night and sleep during the day, you may want to reverse this pattern for awhile.

QUAQUAVERSAL VS. UNILINEAR MINDS. My good friend and fellow spiritual practitioner Genesis P-Orridge has come up with a theory that divides people into two camps based on how they view the universe, due to the way they are "wired": The quaquaversals and the unilinears. The quaquaversals are the original thinkers of the world. The creative minds, the non-conformists, the visionaries. The unilinears are closed-minded, afraid of changes, proestablishment, and rigid. Most spiritual practitioners would have to be by definition quaquaversal. The dictionary defines quaquaversal as *"directed outward from a common center toward all points of the compass; dipping uniformly in all directions."* Unilinear, on the other hand, is described as *"following a single, consistent path of development or progression."* According to Genesis, most people are unilinear and are most active during the daytime, especially between the hours of 9:OOAM to 5:OOPM. Genesis believes that quaquaversal minds can work better at night, when the unilinears are asleep. In the daytime, so much unilinear activity tends to hamper the quaquaversal expansion--the work of the spirit. For this reason, Genesis recommends that most protection rituals and procedures be done at night.

NON-HUMAN ENERGY VAMPIRES. There is a class of demon called incubus and succubus that seeks to copulate with humans. The Bible mentions that before the Great Flood, some demons mated with women, producing a race of supermen called "nefilim." After the Flood, God decreed that these matings of demons and humans would not happen again. These creatures' desire for human flesh, however, did not abate after God's decree. No longer able to openly and materially copulate with humans, these demons now invade their dreams. Because these unnatural demonic trysts can be extremely pleasurable, the human victims at first may not be aware of how serious these attacks can be. Sprinkling holy water on the bed before going to sleep, sprinkling a pinch of sea salt between the sheets, and placing an egg in each of four corners in your bedroom will keep the incubi and succubi away. The eggs must be replaced weekly. Also, most of the treatments offered below also serve to keep these demons away. We will have more on the incubus and sucubus in the next chapter.

II-GENERAL PREVENTIVE MEASURES AND TREATMENT AGAINST ENERGY VAMPIRES

PROTECTIVE BATHS, A POWERFUL MEDICINE. Water is in itself a holy liquid. Without it, no form of life can survive. Add to your bathwater the intangible power of your intention, plus one or several of the tangible psychic protectors available, and you have at your disposal an invaluable ally in your battle against energy vampires. Holy water, spring water, sea water, and water from a sacred source such as the River Jordan can be added to your regular bathwater for protection. Salt, baking soda, camphor, Florida water, white rose petals, and an egg (make sure it doesn't break) are also powerful protectors you can add to your bathwater. Before you enter the bathtub, however, take some water out and save it to use as a floor and wall wash to protect your home.

It is important when taking a spiritual bath to understand that it is different from a regular bath. A normal bath is a necessary sanitary function that removes the dirt and grime of daily living, a spiritual or ritual bath has a totally different aim: to remove unwanted energies and baleful vibrations. The act of undertaking a spiritual bath indicates that the person doing it is a believer in the higher truths. This belief in itself triggers the necessary energies that, mixed with the physical attributes of the ingredients chosen, facilitates the elimination of the unwanted vibrations and the acquisition of positive energies.

Since the primary aim of the spiritual bath is NOT to remove physical dirt, I advise that before taking a spiritual bath you take a good shower to remove all physical dirt, that way you can forget about washing behind the ears etc., and just concentrate on the spiritual aspects of your ritual bath. Although botanicas and other spiritual stores sell prepared baths, I strongly recommend you prepare your own using fresh ingredients whenever applicable.

After adding the necessary ingredient(s) to the bathwater, which should be lukewarm, immerse your nude body totally in the water. Make sure your head is totally immersed, for this is the part of your body that serves as seat of most energies, including the ones you want to get rid of. Ahead I will list some widely-used baths that have been time-tested to work, following that section, I will list herbs to use in your baths that you can choose to make your own baths. Generally speaking, tried and true baths have the advantage of having been tested over years and are more apt to work than new experimentations.

BATHS TO REMOVE NEGATIVITY

BATH ONE

Ingredients
8 ounces of holy water
Petals from eight white roses
1/2 cup of Epsom salts

Add ingredients to half tub of lukewarm water, light a white candle inside bathroom. Concentrate on ridding yourself of all negativity. After about twenty minutes, come out of the bath and pat yourself dry with a clean, white towel.

BATH TWO
Warning: *Do not take this bath*
if your skin is sensitive to ammonia.

Ingredients
1 cup seawater
1 tablespoon ammonia
1 teaspoon Epsom salts

This bath has been in use in the Middle East, with slight variations, since at least the 1300's. Millions of people have benefited from it.

BATH THREE

Ingredients
1 cup milk
1 teaspoon sea salt
Bunch of parsley

While this bath has been used to bring good luck, its original design was to rid a person of negative energies. Goat's milk works better than cow's milk.

BATH FOUR

Ingredients
1 cup Epsom salts
1 teaspoon baking soda
1 cup river water

Mix all ingredients with your bathwater, keep a yellow candle going while you bathe.

BATH FIVE

This bath is the one most Caribbean Spiritualists
prefer for getting rid of bad vibrations.

Ingredients
About 3 ounces of Florida water
1 lump of cascarilla (powdered eggshell)
Petals from five white carnations

After taking bath, take remains of petals and cascarilla and discard far from your home, for it is thought the negativity has been absorbed by these physical remains.

BATHS USED FOR OTHER PURPOSES

BATHS TO INCREASE YOUR WEALTH

BATH ONE

Ingredients
2 loadstones
1 clear quartz
1 whole egg, cracked.

Add everything to your bathwater, remain in tub for half an hour.

BATH TWO

Ingredients
1 bunch of parsley
1 cup of goat's milk
1 stick of cinnamon

Add everything to your bathwater, remain in tub for half an hour.

BATH THREE

Ingredients
Cut three dollar bills up in little pieces,
add pieces to bathwater
7 pennies
1 ounce of myhrr

Add everything to your bathwater, remain in tub for half an hour.

BATH FOUR

Ingredients
One piece High John the Conqueror root
One teaspoon High John the Conqueror oil
Orange blossom cologne

Add everything to bathwater, afterwards, pick up the root from the bathtub and tie a green ribbon around it. Hang it behind your front door to bring wealth to your home.

BATH FIVE

Ingredients
5 cinnamon sticks
5 bags of chamomile tea
1 bunch parsley

Take this bath each Friday for five consecutive Fridays, it will improve your cash flow.

LOVE BATHS

BATH ONE

Ingredients
Petals from five yellow roses
Drop of honey
Five splashes from five different colognes or perfumes
Five cinnamon sticks
Five drops of Florida Water

Mix all ingredients in a large bowl, add water to fill up bowl. Do this on a Tuesday evening, invoking the blessings of Oshun, goddess of love. Leave bowl by a window where the sun will hit it in the early morning, add to bathwater on Wednesday. Do this for five consecutive weeks and you'll see an amazing improvement in your love life.

BATH TWO

Although deceptively simple, this bath is very effective in improving one's love life.

Take five whole oranges, as golden-yellow as possible, add to bathwater, bathe with them, playfully passing the oranges all over your body. Afterwards, take oranges to the river and offer them to the goddess of the river along with five pennies.

BATH THREE

Place six yarrow leaves inside a closed container with distilled water and one teaspoon of sugar. Leave in refrigerator for one week, then add the liquid, not the leaves, to your bathwater while praying for a lover. Works better if done on a Friday evening.

BATH FOUR

Add Come-To-Me oil and Attraction Powder to your bath at least once a week to keep your aura charged with loving vibrations.

BATH FIVE

This bath uncrosses you so you can allow your own charm to come through. Take a whole egg, bathe with it, making sure it doesn't break. Afterwards, take egg to a park and smash against a large tree. Your love life will improve immediately.

HERBS TO USE IN YOUR BATHS

BASIL - Attracts high vibrations. Fills your aura with positive energy, antithetical to the negativity caused by the energy vampire. Add Florida Water to the bath for maximum benefit.

BAY LEAVES (LAUREL) - Makes you immune to attacks. You should also light a white candle in the bathroom while taking the bath. Read 83rd Psalm before entering water for maximum effect.

HYSSOP - Very strong "stripper" of bad energies, should be used with care in baths, but works very well in floor washes. For baths, use only a small quantity and do not stay in the bathtub more than eight minutes, for hyssop can cause headaches if too much of it is used for too long a time.

LETTUCE - Brings clarity and calm.

MINT - Brings a sweet, happy, vibration. Also, a mild aphrodisiac. May not be strong enough for serious energy-depleting attacks. Use as a floor wash before parties to ensure peace and joy.

PARSLEY - Great for attracting wealth. With milk, it also serves as a spiritual restorative. May not be strong enough to fight a very powerful vampire.

PURSLANE - Brings money and the protection of the Mother Goddess.

ROSE PETALS (WHITE) - Excellent bath to keep your aura strong. Eight roses are needed to provide the necessary strength to fight a vampire. Even if you do not feel you are under attack, take this bath once per week, on Thursdays, as a preventive measure.

ROSEMARY - Brings good fortune, but may not be strong enough by itself to stave off an energy vampire's attack. Mix with bay leaves.

RUE - Gather the rue in front of you, by your altar (if you have one). Light a purple candle and, putting your hands over the rue, palms touching the herb, say:

> *"In the name of God the Father, his power the Shekinnah, and their offspring the Chirst, I compel this rue to be ruth, eliminating the ruthless. By the secret name of God, Adonai-Eloim Yaweh-Amen."*

Use some in your baths and floor washes to keep evil away.

SAGE - Works better burned than in baths. Use in baths if specifically told to do so by a spiritual practitioner, or if you were told to do so in a dream.

VERVAIN - Excellent for keeping away psychic attacks.

OTHER INGREDIENTS USED IN BATHS

LAUNDRY BLUEING - Is used in the Caribbean as a revitalizing ingredient in spiritual baths.

BAKING SODA - Is often used in baths by people searching for God's mercy, or by those who seek repentance over bad deeds.

COFFEE - Adding coffee to your bathwater helps you recover from any illness as it strengthens your aura.

NUTS

Although popular among Native Americans, Appalachian folk, and some European practitioners, the use of nuts in baths is not widely known. Nuts can be very powerful ingredients if used correctly. The traditional way of extracting the esoteric benefits nuts offer is by boiling a few nuts in a heavy iron pot for a long time, two hours minimum, replacing the water that evaporates as needed. Use only the liquid in your bath, never the nut itself.

ALMOND - Adding almond to your bathwater makes you more loving and more lovable.

HAZELNUT - Makes you wiser, helps open your third eye.

NUTMEG - Gives you power over others.

PECAN - (not recommended if you eat pecans on a regular basis) Cook pecans in a COPPER rather than an IRON pot, for this nut belongs to Oshun. Adding pecan water to your bath makes you more attractive, but it doesn't always work well if you eat pecans. If in doubt, do not take this bath, for it can cause headaches if done the wrong way.

WALNUT - Is generally used to forget a loved one who has left you, or to speed up the cutting of a painful liaison. Concentrate on your intention while bathing, asking the Universe to rid you of bad relationships.

CANDLES, COLORS, AND THE SIGNS OF THE ZODIAC

Although most of us are aware of how the vibratory frequencies of sound affect us, we are less aware of how visual vibrations--colors-make us feel. Since at least the Middle Ages, astrologers have sought to equate different colors with the different signs of the Zodiac. What follows is a list of signs of the Zodiac and the colors that vibrate harmoniously with each sign. The first color named will be the most harmonious, others listed are also harmonious, but less so.

Aries	Mar. 21 - Apr. 19	White, Rose
Taurus	Apr. 20 - May 19	Red, Yellow
Gemini	May 20 - June 18	Sky Blue, Red
Cancer	June 19 - July 23	Green, Brown
Leo	July 24 - Aug 22	Green, Red
Virgo	Aug. 23 - Sept. 21	Gold, Black speckled with Blue
Libra	Sept. 22 - Oct. 21	Red, Black, Light Blue
Scorpio	Oct. 22 - Nov. 20	Golden Brown, Black
Sagittarius	Nov. 21 - Dec. 20	Green, Gold, Red
Capricorn	Dec. 21 - Jan. 19	Garnet, Blue, Silver, Gray, Black
Aquarius	Jan. 20 - Feb. 18	Blue, Pink, Emerald Green, Black
Pisces	Feb. 19 - Mar. 20	Pink, White, Emerald Green, Black

When lighting a candle for your protection, you can increase the candle's power by choosing one that harmonizes with your birth sign. The proper way to prepare one of these candles is to dress them with the oil corresponding to your sign. Dressing a candle is not as simple as you may think. Candles, like magnets, have polarity. To dress a candle with oil, start from the middle and go up (North), then start in the middle and go South (down). If you were born under the sign of Aries, for example, you'd buy a white or rose-colored candle, and dress it with Aries oil which you can purchase at a botanica or occult store. Burning some Aries incense at the same time would make your protection even stronger.

Certain colors stand for certain qualities. Knowing what colors harmonize with the quality you most wish to bring to your life may help you decide such things as what color to paint your bedroom, your workspace, etc. For example, pale blue induces calmness and pleasant dreams, therefore, you may want to paint your bedroom this color. If you are trying to have a baby, however, you may want your bedroom painted green, since green is the color of growth and fertility. Following are the colors and their correspondences.

DARK BLUE - Depressing, moody, unfortunate, subdued.

LIGHT BLUE - Spiritual understanding, soothing, happiness, coolness of character, protection, good dreams, calm.

BROWN - The color of the earth. Neutral. Non- specific,

CRIMSON - Same as red, with some gold.

GARNET - Same as red, with a little blue.

GOLD - Attraction, magnetic, hypnotic, alluring, cheerful, wealth, born rich, not a care in the world.

GREENISH YELLOW - Jealousy, sickness, cowardice, anger, discord.

GREEN - Growth, wealth, financial success, good crops, healing (do not use to heal cancer, for it promotes growth of anything living, including cancer cells).

MAUVE - Helps you gain the trust of those around you. Increases your sense of self-worth.

ORANGE - A happy mixture of yellow and red, orange clears the mind, improves finances, inspires you to work more and better.

PINK - Passion, success, conquering evil, clean living, anti-addiction, love, honor, friendliness, harmony.

PURPLE - Psychic abilities, deep meditation, overcoming obstacles, color of royalty. A powerful color to work magic with. Wear purple to receive respect, since it is the color of high priests. A purple candle can be used to meditate on raising one's spirituality/consciousness.

RED - Symbolizes love, health, and vigor.

SILVER - Victory of good over evil, death of the devil's minions.

TEAL (a dark grayish-greenish-blue) - Balances your spiritual side with your practical side.

TURQUOISE - Allows workaholics to "slow down and smell the coffee." Identified with Native Americans, turquoise can be used to induce stress-relief, knowledge, and finding logic in situations.

WHITE - Purity, truth, spiritual strength, power, realization, relief of tension, focusing one's goals, clarity, and acceptance. Use white as a substitute for any other color! Good for invoking the Maiden aspect of The Female Deity.

YELLOW - Makes your voice be heard. Persuasive, fascinating color. A good color for working with the element of air, and for invoking the masculine aspects of Deity.

PROTECTION WHILE YOU SLEEP

You are at your most vulnerable while you are asleep. This is the time when energy vampires prefer to strike. If the energy vampire has access to your home, he or she may actually sit by your side while you sleep, actually sucking away your energy in a brazen manner. Sleep time, however, also provides us with the best clues that we are being attacked by an energy vampire. These clues may include one or more of the following symptoms:

- Consistent nightmares
- Waking up feeling tired, even though you've had a full night's sleep.

- Waking up with thoughts alien to you; feeling as if someone else was in your head.

- Waking up with a dull, persistent headache.

- Waking up thinking of someone you wouldn't normally be thinking about.

Praying before going to sleep has been the time-tested method of protection in keeping away demons. Prayers, however, are only as effective as the faith and devotion expressed by the suppliant. For Christians, the Lord's Prayer is the most powerful. It goes like this:

THE LORD'S PRAYER

Our Father, who art in heaven, hollowed be Thy name, Thy kingdom come, Thy will be done, on earth as it is in heaven. Give us this day our daily bread, and forgive us our trespasses as we forgive those who trespass against us, and lead us not into temptation, but deliver us from evil. Amen. [10]

Another ancient Christian prayer of protection before retiring to sleep is the following:

EVENING PRAYER

Now that the day has come to a close, I thank you, O Lord, and entreat that the evening with the night may be without sin, grant this to me, O Savior, and save me. Glory be to the Father and to the Son and to the Holy Spirit. Now that the day has passed, I glorify you, O Master, and entreat that the evening with the night may be without offence; grant this to me, O Savior, and save me. Now and always, and forever and ever. Amen Now that the day has run its course, I praise you, O Holy One, and entreat that the evening with the nightmay be undisturbed, grant this to me, O Savior, and save me.

Practitioners of Wicca and other neo-Pagan faiths tend to be eclectic, gathering their prayers and affirmations from ancient texts, as well as making new ones up. The following is a Wiccan version of an evening prayer:

WICCAN EVENING CHANT

Lord and Lady, twirl about. Guide me day and night, throughout. Guide me through each passing hour And grant me Your protective power. From head to toe, from sky to ground, Keep me safe and well and sound.[11]

The reason I believe Jewish and Roman Catholic/Eastern Orthodox prayers are more effective is because these prayers have been vested with thousands of years of existence, fortified by billions of heartfelt utterances by the faithful. An effective and ancient Christian prayer of protection, which must be performed in a specified fashion, is the Jesus Prayer.

THE JESUS PRAYER

Contrary to popular belief, Christianity does not lack the power of the mantra. While it is obvious that Hinduism and Buddhism have continued to make use of spoken protective mantras much more successfully than traditions stemming from Abraham *(Judaism, Christianity, and Islam)*. One powerful Christian incantation has survived in the Byzantine rite of the Catholic Church, it is called *The Jesus Prayer*, and as its mystic power is being re-discovered in the West, it is becoming more and more popular. The Jesus prayer is the only ancient Christian prayer left that asks that you synchronize your breathing with the invocation of the name of Jesus. In this prayer, you do not have to occupy your thoughts with the content of the prayer (as you would do with a rosary); you are provided with a point of attention which frees your mind to receive the vibratory frequencies of the healing name of Jesus. The result is that the prayer serves to strengthen and protect you at a "not-conscious" level. This powerful invocation has its roots not only in the New Testament, but even further back in the Old Testament, where we see a developed personal conviction that the invocation of the name of God brings with it the conscious realization of His presence: *"Call on my name, I will hear" (Zec. 13: 9).* Once a year, on the day of Atonement, Yahweh's name was pronounced only by the high priest who was chosen to offer sacrifice inside the "Holy of Holies" of the temple in Jerusalem. In the New Testament, there is ample evidence of the power that emanates from the reverent pronouncing of the name of Jesus. Philippians 2: 9-10 tells us that *"God has given Him a name that is above all names so that at the name of Jesus every knee shall bend in heaven, on earth, and under the earth."* Lost in the beginnings of Christianity, the Jesus Prayer became a powerful mantra when executed as follows. After taking a deep breath, you say: LORD, JESUS CHRIST. Then, after softly exhaling, you say: SON OF GOD. Again, you take a deep breath and say, HAVE MERCY ON ME. Then you exhale and say A SINNER. On a set of beads designed for this purpose, called "Jesus beads," you count the times you say the prayer, which gives you more power the more times you repeat it. Notice that you are inhaling, TAKING IN, the Holy Name, while exhaling, THROWING OUT, your own sinful nature. This simple exercise allows angelic, high vibrations to permeate your being while expelling negative, low vibrations sent to you by a psychic attacker.

THE JESUS PRAYER

Lord Jesus Christ
Son of God
Have mercy on me,
a sinner.

You can also write the prayer on parchment using dragon's blood ink, place parchment in a red flannel bag, dress with sacramental oil or holy water, and keep with you at all times for constant protection.

ACTIVELY ATTACKING THE VAMPIRE

Sun Tzu, legendary Chinese strategist, said that the best defense is a good offense. Actively defending yourself and your loved ones from the attacks of a psychic vampire may prove to be the most effective method of dealing with such a situation In most cases, you will be aware of who the energy vampire is. It is that person who "drains you" after you've spoken to him for a while. That person who you've been dreaming about, even though you don't particularly like him. If the energy vampire has been trying to influence your thoughts, you will wake up with thoughts foreign to you. Let's say you are a boss and you are thinking of firing a particularly useless employee. All of a sudden, you begin to wake up thinking, "so-and-so isn't that bad!" Until, much to your detriment, you forget to fire this problem-causing leach! One of the most insidious attacks comes from someone who uses an incubus or a succubus to sexually attack you while you are asleep. Anyone who gets a hold of one of the grimoires popularized in Europe in the 19th century can potentially release certain demons from their astral restraints. A whole class of demons called incubi and succubi exist solely to experience sexual intercourse with humans. Although the attack of these demons has historically been considered a nuisance rather than a serious threat, if left untreated these episodes can prove draining on the human. Repeated attacks by sexual demons may cause you to feel debased, unnatural, and unworthy of higher spiritual pursuits.

The person using a demon to influence you sexually will usually perform a ritual giving the demon his visage. Since these demons are generally experts at giving sexual pleasure, especially making use of so-called "deviant" sexual practices, the idea is that you come to believe that you have experienced an astral sexual encounter with the person the demon is impersonating, making you more likely to accept the idea of having sex with him or her in the material plane!

AMERICAN INDIAN FEATHER COUNTERATTACK

Based on a Native American custom first observed among different groups in the Pacific Northwest, This procedure has been adopted by

Wiccans and other neo-Pagans in the twentieth century.

STEP 1   Obtain a feather from a bird of prey. If not in the wild, then from a zoo.

STEP 2   Get a seven-day pull out candle in the color of the energy vampire's sign. If unknown, use a white one.

STEP 3   Dress the candle with Patchouli oil.

STEP 4   Tie feather to side of candle using 50 feet of black thread.

STEP 5   Take the prepared candle to a spot away from your house, a clearing in the forest or a motel room in Newark, whichever is applicable to your particular geographical situation

STEP 6   Put all ingredients in the middle of a circle at least nine feet wide. Add a stamped envelope, a red ink pen, and a sheet of paper to the prepared candle. Mark the outline of the circle using pembe or cascarilla chalk.

STEP 7   At midnight or 3:00 AM, light the candle and, facing South, with sincere intent, and palms facing up, say: *"Lords of Karma, to my needs tend. This cursed attack must hereby end!"* Slowly and ceremoniously walk counterclockwise (withershins) to the East position and, this time with arms extended in front of you, palms facing down, say: *"Your familiar I have slain, you will feel continuous pain".* Walk to the North position and say: *"because you failed in your dharma, I call upon you instant karma!"* Finally, in the West position, prick your skin with a sanitized needle, let a drop of your blood fall inside the circle, and say: *"With my own life seal I this pact, I now expect my God to act. Consumatum est, Consumatum est, Consumatum est, Amen!*

STEP 8 Erase circle with your left foot using a clockwise motion. Collect all ingredients. Before you go back home, take candle and relight near or in a cemetery, in as secluded a spot as possible, remove the feather, place feather and black thread inside envelope, write the following note on the paper using red ink. *"After all is said and done, your power over me is gone."* Write name of vampire here, address the envelope to him or her, and send it to his/her address. DO NOT PUT YOUR NAME OR RETURN ADDRESS ANYWHERE. This energy vampire will never bother you again.

ANOTHER COUNTERATTACK

Gather the following ingredients:

Pigeon excrement • Gunpowder • Black Pepper
Seven dead fleas or ticks
Pencil, Parchment paper or Brown paper bag
Prayer of St. Alex
Black seven-day candle
Pembe chalk, Cascarilla, or regular white chalk

STEP 1 Get the pigeon excrement, a teaspoonful of gunpowder, a teaspoonful of black pepper, and the seven dead fleas or ticks; mix all these ingredients together.

STEP 2 With the pencil, write the name of the energy vampire on the parchment or on a brown paper bag.

STEP 3 Set paper on fire, making sure all ashes remain.

STEP 4 Add ashes to mixture. Put everything inside a glass container that has a cover, such as a small jar.

STEP 5 At the hour of midnight, draw an inverted pentagram using pembe chalk, cascarilla, or any white chalk on the floor. Light black candle, set on bottom point of pentagram, which should be pointing south.

STEP 6   Sit naked on the floor, the black candle between your open legs. Put jar containing mixture in the middle of the pentagram. Read prayer to San Alex three times.

STEP 7   Stand up, shake jar vigorously so all ingredients become well mixed. Remove half the mixture, which should be like a black powder, and save inside an envelope.

STEP 8   Put your clothes back on, leave candle burning , take jar with remaining mixture to a cemetery. Throw jar over cemetery gate along with nine pennies while saying *"Hekua Yansan, I'm not ready for your big house yet!"*

STEP 9   The next day, blow remainder of mixture on the person if possible, or by a place he or she will visit. Before the seven-day candle is done, the person will have ceased to be a problem for you!

Chapter 5
NEGATIVE SPACES
& HAUNTING PLACES

I - DEFINING THE NEGATIVE SPACE

WHAT IS A NEGATIVELY CHARGED SPACE? Vibrations which are negatively experienced by people cling to certain spaces due to several causes. For example, in the introduction I spoke of a building a friend of a friend was purchasing, so filled with negativity that I could literally hear the anguished cries of thousands of murdered babies (the place was a 19th century abortion mill where late-term abortions were routinely done). The pain and horror felt by all those women, the terrible fate of those fetuses, the greed and callousness of the abortionists all converged to cause such an overflow of negativity that some of it must have become affixed to the place, same way you can walk into an old, abandoned, coffee plantation building and still smell the coffee.

In certain west African ports that were points of departure for slaves, there are buildings still standing that were used as holding cells for the unfortunate victims of the slave trade. Today, even after so much time has elapsed, one can still feel the anguish of these souls when one walks into one of these buildings. Other sites, while not necessarily evil, are charged with the wrong kind of energy for everyday living, such as when houses are built on top of burial grounds or on sacred Native American spaces. Another way a person can receive negative karma from a place is if he or she takes something away from a sacred site without permission. This is the case with many tourists in Hawaii who take souvenir lava rocks from certain volcanoes only to find themselves later facing a string of bad luck. If this last thing happens, the remedy is easy: send the "souvenir" back to the place! In Hawaii, the post office nearest the volcano where you picked up the piece is used to handling returned rocks from tourists who leave no return address on the packages. The reason why taking something from a sacred space may carry some negativity has to do with the concept of manna. *"Manna"* is a force inherent in the universe that is the psychic equivalent of electricity. Manna is like electricity; properly used, it can be a great help to humanity. Improperly used, however, manna, like electricity, can kill you. It is believed that certain places and certain individuals are so charged with manna that the average human can become sick or even die if he or she does not take certain precautions when being exposed to the powerful retainer of manna, whether it is a place or a person.

Another way a place can become "haunted" is by having been cursed either by a practitioner of evil magic, or by someone righteous who suffered a great injustice at the place. In the city of Matanzas, in the island-nation called Cuba, there is a large tract of land that looks out of place in the middle of a rich sugar cane plantation; it is dry and totally devoid of any visible life. Scientists are at a loss to explain the phenomenon of this mini-desert amidst some of the lushest vegetation in the world. To the locals this is no mystery; Hatuey, a powerful Native American[12] chief, was burned at the stake in the center of that spot nearly five centuries ago. In fact, the word "Matanzas" is the plural of the Spanish matanza, which means slaughter or massacre, a name given to the place because of the great numbers of Native Americans massacred by the Spaniards there. History says that when Hatuey was burning at the stake Father Bartolome de Las Casas propped a crucifix in front of Hatuey's face calling out "Accept Jesus, my son! Accept him now that you may go to heaven!" To which Hatuey replied, "Do the white folk go to heaven?" "Sure," the priest said, "heaven does not discriminate." At this point Hatuey made a remark for which he would always be remembered, he said: "If the whites who have destroyed my land and my people are going to heaven, I much prefer to go to hell!" According to local lore, it was at this time that Hatuey looked up and said "Let nothing ever grow here so that all can see they've killed a righteous man!" Today, nothing remains in a circle measuring about fifty feet except the charred tree stump where Chief Hatuey was murdered.

II-REMOVING THE NEGATIVE ENERGY

CLEANSING OF A DWELLING. After you have removed the negative vibrations that pestered your person, you may want to make sure all of it is gone by treating the place where you dwell. I wouldn't be surprised if some of the negative energy sent to you attached itself to your home. Cleansing a home is a multi-level endeavor. The first and most important step towards having a psychically-cleared home is to make sure all who live under the same roof, as well as those who visit often, are free of rancor and bad feelings towards each other. Negativity feeds on arguments and conflicts. After the initial step of striving to maintain an atmosphere of peace, take the necessary steps as follows:

STEP 1   Make sure all who live under the same roof are in harmony; avoid arguments and conflicts.

STEP 2   In the pail you use for mop water, add a dozen ice cubes, 1/2 cup of ammonia, and one tablespoon sea salt to the water. Remove one cup of the mixture from the pail, you will use this later to sponge the walls with.

STEP 3   Although this next step may seem disgusting to you, it is imperative that you overcome your distaste for this practice, for its benefits are enormous. Have everyone who lives with you deposit a drop of his/her own urine in the mop water--something you should also do, of course.

STEP 4   Starting from the back of the house, mop every room that can be mopped. In rooms where you have carpets and rugs, use a barely damp mop and gently go over the floor. Take remaining mop water to the street and dump.

STEP 5   With a new sponge, gently dip in cup of prepared water you had set apart earlier, the same as the mop water minus the urine, and sponge at least some part of each wall. Start from the back to the front. Flush remainder of water down the toilet while saying *"All negativity leaves with this water."*

STEP 6   Place a seven-day black candle, dressed with unhexing oil, in each room of the house. Light candles and pray 23rd Psalm each night for seven nights. At the end, throw all remainders of candles in a river, along with five pennies. House will now be cleared of all negative energy.

CLEARING A SPACE USING EGGS

Place an egg in each corner of each room that is to be cleared of negative energy. Wait 21 days, gather all eggs and smash inside a cemetery.

In Santeria, Obeah, Vodou, and all other Afro-Diasporic religious expressions, eggs are used to pick up negative energy. Practitioners of evil use these eggs that have picked up negative energy to curse others, by simply throwing these negatively-charged eggs on the gates or doorways of the homes of targeted victims. In one of Cuba's most famous films, Plaff! (Splat!), the psychological result of this type of egg-throwing is portrayed in a semi-comical fashion--at the end, it is discovered that the egg that destroyed the protagonist, played by brilliant Cuban actress Daisy

Granados, was inadvertently thrown by herself!

Appalachian practitioners, Wiccans, ceremonial magicians, and many others use eggs in a remarkably similar fashion. The famous Gypsy trick of passing an egg over a person in order to cleanse that person then breaking the egg to find blood or some foul-smelling black substance in it is not always a trick! I know this because I once cleansed my own brother using an egg and, when I broke the egg, which I had purchased that same day, it was full of foul-smelling blood!

CLEARING YOURSELF AFTER HAVING DESECRATED A SACRED SITE. If you removed an object from a sacred site, make sure the object is returned, then light a white candle to the guardians of the site, asking them to forgive you and leave you in peace. If you have access to a holy person, or a priesthood holder, in the tradition you have desecrated, make contact with that person and make amends. My brother once bought property in what had been an Indian burial ground. He and his family had no rest until they contacted a local medicine man who led them in a series of appeasement rituals that worked. They've had no other problems since then, about twenty years ago.

CLEARING NEGATIVITY WITH WATER. Get used to the routine of filling a clear glass with water before going to sleep, putting the glass under your bed or by your head, and flushing it down the toilet each morning. This simple ritual serves as a powerful guard against negative energy. It also helps keep at bay the spirits of the dead. Adding sea salt to the water makes it even stronger.

You can also sprinkle a pinch of sea salt between your sheets, in the corners of your bedroom, and by each doorway in your home to keep negativity away. Angelica root and camphor serve the same purpose.

III - UNWANTED VISITS FROM THE DEAD

KEEPING THE DEAD AWAY. I have been a spirit medium for thirty-eight years. Communicating with the dead is as natural to me as communicating with the living. But I realize that such encounters can be unnerving and even traumatic to most people. If you are being visited by a Catholic relative or friend who died, have a priest say nine masses for that person in your name, and you may pray a novena in his or her memory. Cascarilla, a chalky substance made out of dried eggshells, is antithetical to the dead. Drawing crosses with it behind windows and doorways keeps the spirits of the departed away. Keeping an ancestor altar helps maintain a good balance in most people's homes. This may be done by covering a small table with a white cloth, placing seven clear glasses filled with water on top, along with pictures of dead friends and relatives and religious symbols such as crosses displayed on the altar. Keeping a Bible open to the 23rd Psalm or the Lord's Prayer also keeps the dead away. When we speak of "the dead," we may be speaking of different kinds of energies. One is the psychic imprint left by someone who either died unexpectedly, had a lot of power, or was killed in a violent fashion. This "empty hull" may simply be a powerful image, not a sentient being. A holograph, if you will. The other energy is that of an intelligence that has left the material plane but has not yet reached its next stage. In more rare cases, the "dead" may in fact be souls in heaven who come down to guide us. These are called variously "guiding spirits," "saints," or "boddhisattvas." In any case, the inexperienced should avoid all contact with the dead, leaving such endeavors to the seasoned practitioner.

Chapter 6
PROTECTION WITH SAINTS

I - OLD GODS, NEW SAINTS

THE DEMISE OF PAGANISM AND THE RISE OF CHRISTIANITY. As Christianity, then a branch of fiercely monotheistic Judaism, began to make inroads into Pagan Europe, the Old Gods began to be persecuted and destroyed with the same zeal Pagans had once persecuted Christians. People who for centuries had depended on different deities to heal different maladies for a time found themselves shorn of their celestial benefactors. This situation did not last long, however, for the old gods re-emerged under the guise pious Christian saints! These "saints by acclamation," many never receiving official recognition by formal canonization, include St. Bridget of Kildare, who replaced the goddess Brighid, St. Tharteus, who replaced Cernunnos, and St. Barbara, who replaced Mars, god of war. In 1968 Pope Paul VI removed these and many other saints of dubious origins from the official calendar of saints of the Roman Catholic Church, but he added that those who continued to venerate these saints would not be found guilty of any wrongdoing.

In Catholic countries such as Mexico, Haiti, and Cuba indigenous practitioners work extensively with the imagery of Catholic saints. Recently, even neo-Pagans, Wiccans, and "New Agers" have discovered the power of these saints. Following are some of the more popular saints and how to invoke their protection. I believe that when addressing these archetypes at the level of sincere worship, official Church dogma has nothing to say, and anyone, whether Catholic or not, can access the power of these saints.

SAINT ALEX (ALEJO)
Light a pink candle to his image every Sunday to keep away enemies.

PRAYER TO ST. ALEX

Oh glorious St. Alex mine! You who have the power to chase away all the evil that preys on the chosen of the Lord, I ask that you chase away my enemies.

Chase Satan away from me, chase liars and sorcerers away from me. Also, chase away sin and, lastly, Chase away all who would come to cause me harm. Get me so far from the bad ones that they'll never be able to see me. So it is.

Chase away any ill-thinking mortal. chase away those unthinking fools who would harm me. bring me close to the Lord so that with his divine grace he will cover me with goodness and reserve a spot for me under the shadow of the Holy Spirit, Amen, Jesus.

ST. BARBARA

Place a small metal sword in an upright position next to her image. Light a red candle to her and ask her to protect you from all harm. Do this every Saturday.

PRAYER TO ST. BARBARA

Oh Holy Christian protector, with your cloak protect me, save me from all harm. Bless me with your hands and strengthen me with your faith. Guide me, guard me and protect me from enemies and evil temptations. Protect my house and all that surrounds it from evil influences, envy, jealousy and faithlessness. Amen.

OUR LADY OF FATIMA

Protects from evil, turns back psychic attacks, place her picture in a frame, hang it high above your bed. Light a white candle and offer her white flowers. Do this every Tuesday and she'll keep your house free of negative energy.

ST. MICHAEL THE ARCHANGEL
Light three candles to his image every Tuesday, one red, one purple, one green, to protect your home.

PRAYER TO ST. MICHAEL

God and Lord of the angels, to whom you entreat the welfare of man. I offer you the merits of these Sovereign Spirits and of the Prince of Angels, who himself and with help from his ministers guards human nature, so you may guard me of all sin and grant me an angelic purity.

Most glorious prince of the heavenly court, Most Excellent Archangel St. Michael, Great Prime Minister of God, friend of Jesus Christ and most favored of his most holy mother, defender of the Church and advocate of man, Since so much do you favor your devotees, help me learn to love and serve them also, and bring to me from the Lord that which I desire and request in this prayer, for your greater glory and honor, and benefit to my soul, Amen.

ST. PETER

Light a red candle and a white candle to his image on Tuesdays to remove obstacles from your life.

PRAYER TO ST. PETER

Glorious King of the Apostles to whom our Lord Jesus Christ spoke first after his glorious and wonderful resurrection. We beg you to grant us the grace that the Lord designated you to give us, and for the intimate thoughts of your conscience. To think about us poor people and forgive us our faults, Glorious Saint Peter and grant us this grace so that we can purify our souls by means of true pain and cleanse ourselves of everything that has offended you. Grant that by the help of this intercession, we may be released from the bonds of our sins. Amen.

ST. THERESE OF LISIEUX

Light a yellow candle to her image every Wednesday to keep away the evil eye.

ST. LUCY

Keep a pair of tiny gold eyes on a dish near your baby's crib as protection against evil eye. Wear them on a chain as protection for your eyesight. Candle: White Day: Wednesday.

PRAYER TO ST. LUCY
SPECIAL ADVOCATE FOR THE EYES

Oh Glorious Virgin and Martyr St. Lucy Who was blessed from infancy by being chosen by the Eternal Father as his worthy daughter, By the Sovereign Son as his beloved Spouse, and by the Holy Ghost as his pleasant abode! I beseech you, my Saint, grant me from the Most Blessed Trinity the ability to express a most fervent devotion. Just as your most fortunate soul was able to glorify God, it being inflamed with the ardor of love for Him, never wavering from such a noble pursuit, until your soul attained two crowns, Virgin and Martyr, may I also attain, with your potent intercession, the ability to love Him in Truth, so that when this life is spent after having served and loved Him, I may be given the privilege of seeing his Glorious Joy in the blessed assurance of the next life, Amen.

With your most precious eyes Look after me, comely Virgin, As I am most humbly urging, free me from unhealthy ties. Oh Lucy, if through your trials You kept your eyes on the dove Keep my eyes safe with love and I'll walk the extra miles.

(at this point, make your request and say three Our Fathers and three Hail Marys)

ST. FRANCIS OF ASSISI
Light a brown candle to his image on Mondays to bring love to the homefront.

PRAYER OF ST. FRANCIS

My Lord Jesus, Light and Splendor of The Eternal Father, you who with so many lights illustrated the seraphic St. Francis, defending him against the hellish hordes that sought to destroy him, I implore, oh Lord, that you may enlighten my thoughts so that I'll be able to recognize the sins that against your divine majesty I've committed, and that by with a contrite heart confessing them, I may be freed from the demons that would wish me to fall. Help me so I may dedicate my life and death to you, Amen.

ST. PAUL
Light a blue candle, and a white one to his image on Tuesdays to calm a restless home.

ST. CHRISTOPHER

Light a purple candle to his image on Saturdays to obtain protection from all evil. He'll "carry" you when you've become exhausted.

PRAYER TO ST. CHRISTOPHER

Grant the following to those who invoke you, glorious Martyr Saint Christopher, allow them to be preserved from epidemics, and earthquakes, from the rages of storms, fires, and floods. Protect us with your intercession during life from the calamities that Providence may hold for us. During death free us from convictions, assisting us during the last hour, that we may reach eternal good will. Amen.

ST. RITA OF CASCIA

Light a white candle to her image on Sundays to keep evil at bay.

SAINT EXPEDITUS
Light a yellow candle to his image every Thursday to make your problems dissolve fast and your enemies be defeated soon.

PRAYER TO ST. EXPEDITUS

Oh glorious Martyr and protecting Saint of ours, Saint Expeditus, having faith in your great merits and above all in the precious blood of Jesus Christ. We humbly beg of you to reach out to us and send us from God the necessary virtues to make us good and pious. And by studying and exercising your virtues, we can practice them and follow your example here in life so that we can deserve the merits of glory. Amen.

ST. NORBERT
Light a brown candle to his image on Tuesdays to stay grounded.

GUARDIAN ANGEL
Light a white candle to his image on Mondays to keep you safe.

PRAYER TO THE GUARDIAN ANGEL

Oh protector spirit who incessantly watches over me; You who have received this mission because you enjoy doing good works and you need to do it so your soul will advance; save me! During the night, when my spirit wanders through unknown passages, guide me safely to friends and loved ones, and those who would teach me lessons and grant me counsel useful to my living which I'll enact tomorrow. Guide my soul through Nature, help me contemplate it and lift my soul above those new challenges that could make me lose all hope. Amen.

ST. RAPHAEL
Light a pink candle to his image on Monday to dispel evil spirits and restore good health.

ST. LOUIS BELTRAN
Keep his image near you at all times. Most potent fighter against evil eye. See page 20 for his prayer.

ST. BENEDICT
Light a white candle to his image on Saturdays for protection against evil, fevers, temptations, and contagious diseases.

OUR LADY OF MERCY
Light a white candle to her image on Sundays to keep troubles away and harmony in the home.

II-EFFICACIOUS POPULAR SAINTS OF THE CARIBBEAN

The majority of these saints are not recognized by the Catholic Church, but their intercession has proven enormously helpful through hundreds of years.

SEVEN AFRICAN POWERS
Light a seven-color, 7-day candle on Monday next to the image of the Seven African Powers to keep your home free of negative vibrations. Read *Prayer to the Seven African Powers* out loud next to lit candle if you feel you are being attacked.

PRAYER OF THE SEVEN AFRICAN POWERS

Oh, Seven Powers that are saints among saints!
Humbly I kneel before your miraculous image,
asking for your help before God.
Oh Heavenly Father who protects us all when we are happy or sad,
I ask you in the name of Almighty Jesus Christ
for this petition (say your request).
Now, once again I have peace of mind and material prosperity.
Keep away from my house all harm and evil which may cause me hardship.
May they never return. My heart tells me this petition
is just and will be granted, if granted, it will glorify your name forever
Jesus Christ in the name of the Father, Son, and Holy Ghost.
Listen, Shango! I call upon you, Oshun! Help me, Yemaya!
Look upon me with grace, Obatala! Come to me. Ogun!
Be good to me, Orula! Intercede for me, Eleggua!
All Seven African Powers in the name of Olofi, grant my request!
(make sign of the cross)

POWERFUL HAND OF GOD
Light a multi-colored candle
to the Hand on Mondays to
turn back evil that has been
sent to you. Read the prayer
in times of special need.

PRAYER TO THE POWERFUL HAND OF GOD
(Say your request, then read the prayer)

*Here I come with the faith
of a Christian soul looking for your mercy
while under such anguished circumstances.
Leave me not without your shelter.
If a door opens to me that would not serve me,
let it be your Powerful Hand that shuts it for me!
And if such door leads to my happiness
and peace I have longed for,
then by all means leave it open.
At your feet I leave this plea, from a soul so hurt by fate
that without your Powerful Hand it cannot think of fighting.
Oh God, please forgive any fault I may possess
and grant me strength that I may yet triumph
for your honor and glory,
Our Father, who art in heaven...*

LONELY SOUL OF PURGATORY
Light a red & black candle to
the Lonely Soul on Mondays
to turn back evil that has
been sent to you. Read her
prayer out loud if you feel
you are being attacked.

PRAYER TO THE LONELY SOUL

Sad Soul, Lonely Soul.
No one mentions your name.
I love you, I call upon you.
No one needs you, I need you!
No one loves you because you cannot enter heaven,
since you are in purgatory.
Get on a fine horse and go to the forest,
from a tree you know well you will cut three branches.
One you'll give to the Spirit that Overcomes,
the other to the Spirit that can't rest.
The third one you'll use to make _____ unhappy
until he comes to me, surrendered and shamed.
Until he comes to me, he won't be able to sit, or stand,
or lie down, or recline.
He won't be able to lie with Asian or Black, with White or Brown,
until he humbly comes to me.
Our Father...

ST. ELIAS
Baron of the Cemetery
Light a reversed black candle to him on Saturdays to send back evil that has been sent to you. Read prayer for extra strength.

Prayer to
ST. ELIAS
Baron of the Cemetery

Oh Chosen Lord of the Cemetery!
I invoke your Holy Name three times
so that with the strength of Samson you help me,
or send your most trusted helpers to aid me,
so that no man or woman,
spirit or elemental, may work against me!
That earthly tribunals will be unable
to judge or condemn me!
And that whatever evil is directed against me
be returned to its source!
And may I see my enemy at my door,
humbled and sorry.
Amen.

(this prayer is to be said three times in a row at midnight, under
the light of a candle lit from the bottom so it burns in reverse)

Servant of God,
DR. JOSE GREGORIO HERNANDEZ
Light a white candle to his image and say three Our Fathers to his name on Sundays to maintain good health and peace in the home.

PRAYER TO THE
SERVANT OF GOD
JOSE GREGORIO HERNANDEZ

Oh Lord, My God!
You who are omnipotent and have
taken into your bosom our beloved
Jose Gregorio Hernandez,
to whom you gave by your great mercy
the power to heal the sick in this world,
give him now the power to heal me,
as a spirit doctor, of the maladies that torment
my soul and my being,
if this be to your honor and glory.
I ask this in the name of your Son,
who taught us to pray thus:
Our Father, who art in heaven . . . etc.

ST. MARTHA THE DOMINATRIX.
Light a green candle to her
image on a Friday to keep
an enemy down or make a
wandering husband return.

PRAYER TO ST. MARTHA

Saint Martha, Virgin.
For the food I'll consume today,
for the oil employed in the cleansing of Holy Unction,
I light this green candle to you so you
may remedy my necessities and aid me
in my misery and make me triumph over all of my difficulties,
just as you triumphed over the fierce beasts
you have at your feet.
For you, there are no impossibilities.
Give me health and work so I may
cover my needs and miseries.
Santa Marta,
hear me, tend to me,
for the love of God.
Amen.

PRAYER TO THE JUST JUDGE

(This is one of the Latin practitioner's most important prayers. It is said that no one carrying this prayer in his person can be arrested, suffer an accident, or meet an early death)

He who this prayer with his person brings,
will never fall prey to a wasp's poisoned sting,
temptations will fall by his way like old trees,
and he'll never be called by the menace police.
Women will bring forth their progeny finely,
a man will grow old well respected and manly.

Creed to the Great Power of God, Hail Most Holy Mary

Our faith saves us,
Our faith enlightens us,
Our faith gives us victory over our enemies.

NOTE: Many of these prayers can be found in
Original Publication's "Helping Yourself with Selected Prayers"

JUST JUDGE

Most Holy, Most Blessed, Most fortunate Emblem
where that Just and Pious Judge died.
Your mercy I seek as I ask that you make me
triumph over my enemies and you free me from all demons,
those who are lawmakers and slanderers also.
Most Sacred Sacrament, with two I you see,
with Three I you tie,
to the Father and the Son and the Holy Ghost.

In the Garden of Desires, with the Spirit of God,
to the Just Judge John spoke thus:

Lord, my enemies I see approach.
Let them come, for their feet are tied,
their hands bound, and their eyes blinded.
And as they are powerless with thee,
so shall they be with me and with
all those who were with you.
If eyes they have, they shall not see.
If hands they have, useless against thee,
If mouth they have, they shan't speak to thee,
and if feet they have, they'll never catch up with thee.
It is Holy Mary's invincible power that covers
the innocent like a loving shower.
Make my enemies to a chair of pain be seated,
just as the Lord to the true cross submitted.
Oh my Lord, who shall I trust?
The Virgin Mary I do, of course.
As I trust the Most Holy wafer.
Holy Mother, clean me of sod,
as you freed Jonah from a fish,
for the love of God.

(Say a creed at this point)

ST. MARTIN OF TOURS
Light a red candle to his
image on Tuesdays to
keep away enemies.

ST. BARTHOLOMEW
Light a red candle to his
image on Tuesdays to
obtain protection from violence.

ST. IGNATIUS LOYOLA
Light a white candle to his
image every Saturday to
keep away evil spirits.

FRANCISCO & FRANCISCA
Try to obtain small
figures representing them.
Light a white candle to them
and offer them rum and
cigar smoke to obtain their favor.

III - LATIN AMERICAN ARCHETYPAL IMAGES

Besides working with popular Catholic saints, Latin American practitioners also work with saint-like archetypal images of indigenous semi-deities. These have proven to be excellent protectors.

ESPIRITU CONGO
Light a white candle to his image on Mondays for protection.

Prayer to
THE CONGO SPIRIT

Oh Divine redeemer from the Congo,
Oh Divine redeemer from the Congo,
Oh Divine redeemer from the Congo,
You who have suffered every ignominy,
I beg of you not to allow the same to occur to me, oh friend.
May my mate remain true, May my belief not be threatened,
May you guide my every step,
May all bad things stay away and all good people come my way.
Grant me luck in all my endeavors.
Peace at work and in the street,
and keep my family on the straight path.

(say two Hail Marys now)

NEGRO FELIPE
Light a white candle to his image on Mondays for protection.

PRAYER OF NEGRO FELIPE

*Felipe, wise slave who came from Guinea to Venezuela
by God sent and by the Virgin protected.
As a slave you proved a saint,
and they had to let you go.
Now I ask that you make impotent all
who would enslave me, mind, body and spirit.
Give me your proven blessing. Give me your proven luck.
Keep away all manner of witchcraft, evil eye, and bad luck.*

*In the name of God. Amen.
(say three Our Fathers and two Hail Marys)*

MARIA LIONZA
Light a pink candle to her image on Tuesdays, offer her rum, roses, and cigar smoke. Ask for all kinds of protection.

EL INDIO

(There are several variations of the American Indian archetype, but all are conceived as noble warriors) light a white candle to his image, offer him cigar smoke and rum. Ask for anything, but always be true to whatever you promised!

PRAYER TO EL INDIO

Oh great chief, most loyal Indian spirit
who watches over your home like an eagle.
In the name of the Father, and of the Son, and of the Holy Spirit
I, a devoted believer in your power,
invoke you in this moment of much need
since your native mind understands the suffering of my flesh
and can intercede with Our Eternal Father and confer
upon me your most blessed and divine protection.

Oh, great Indian spirit,
you who are in charge of my protection, I ask in the name of Jesus ,
that with your stone hatchet you break the chains that bind me,
both material and ethereal.
With your poisoned arrow, oh great Indian spirit,
slay all evil thought that has been thrown my way.

Oh great Indian spirit.
With your eagle eyes continue to watch my path.
Let no sorcery, candle, lamp, or bad thought
harm my body or my spirit.

Oh great Indian spirit,
I light this candle in appreciation for your protection,
for your enlightenment and continued advancement, Amen.

CHANGO MACHO

Orange and black candle. Honor him on Fridays by giving his image an apple, a glass of red wine, a candle, and alit cigar. Gives protection from all evil. Place his image next to St. Barbara's.

PRAYER TO CHANGO MACHO

!Chango, my father!
Gaze upon me, protect me,
Keep away all evil spirits and bring
joy and happiness to my home.
Remember I am your child,
and that my home is your home.
Good health please bring to our home.
I thank you my blessed lord.

(Chango's image should go with
St. Barbara's for more protection)

LA MADAMA
Light a white candle to her image and give her a glass of water, some black coffee, and a lit cigar. Ask her for protection.

PRAYER TO LA MADAMA

Oh Glorious Black Mother
whose heart is pure,
I beg of you to calm my needs and
help me emerge victorious over life's challenges.
Teach me to survive,
oh spirit called La Madama,
give me valor and give me strength,
fill me with your vibration so no evil may reach me.
Grant me a little of your much
guarded treasure knowing that where
you are money has no value.
I implore you accede
to be my protectress,
Amen.

(Say three Our Fathers and
two Hail Marys right after)

HERMANO JOSE
Light a multi-colored candle to his image for protection. Wear his "Star of Jose" for protection against all spiritual evil.

PRAYER TO EL HERMANO JOSE

Benevolent and thoughtful spirit of
El Hermano Jose.
Messenger of the Almighty, loving sentinel charged
with the mission of helping us grow in wisdom and love,
we ask that you give us your support
as we face each day's decisions.
Help us, oh loving guide,
have the fortitude of character to
resist harmful thoughts and the temptation
to listen to those misguided spirits that would induce us to err.
Illuminate our thoughts and help us to recognize our defects,
remove the veil of ignorance from our eyes
so that we may recognize our faults.
To you, El Hermano Jose,
who we acknowledge as our guide,
and to all the other good spirits who
take an interest in our well being,
we pray that we may be worthy of your consideration.
You know our needs, we therefore ask that you
improve our lives as we come closer
to being Divine, Amen.

Chapter 7
MAGICAL RITUALS
FOR PROTECTION

PROTECT YOURSELF FROM A HEX

On a Full Moon night blend:

1 pinch of Thyme	*7 tsp. Garlic powder*
7 tsp. Basil	*7 tsp. Parsley leaves*
7 tsp. Sage	*7 drops Protection oil*
1 pinch Salt Peter	

1. Blend mixture well in a wooden bowl on a Tuesday.

2. Put a portion of the mixture in a mojo bag anointed with Jinx Removing oil and carry it with you.

3. Take a bath in the same mixture while burning a Reversing candle and some Jinx Removing incense.

4. Burn Jinx Removing incense daily in the home.

This procedure will uncross any hexed person and will protect from being hexed for 7 weeks. The procedure may be repeated.

TO LIFT A HEX, BREAK UP BAD CONDITIONS OR TO REMOVE A JINX OR HOODOO

Best performed on a Wednesday when the moon is waxing.

1. In your bathroom, light three yellow candles and some Jinx Removing incense.

2. Put a tablespoon of Van-Van Bath Crystals in your hot bath water. Bathe for about 20 minutes as you meditate on being free of all that is bad and ruining your life.

3. After the bath, anoint yourself on the heart, head and hands with Uncrossing oil. Put the candles out.

4. The following Saturday, light a purple candle and anoint your brow with the oil and recite Psalm 91 from the bible.

5. Repeat this ritual each Wednesday and Saturday until the hex or crossed conditions are lifted from your life.

PEACEFUL HOME SPELL

Begin on a day of the New Moon.

> *High John the Conqueror incense*
> *Helping Hand incense*
> *1 blue candle*
> *1 parchment paper*
> *1 Peaceful Home oil*

1. Anoint the candle with the oil and write the word "Peace" nine times on the square of parchment. Set that beneath the candle.

2. Light a bit of the High John incense and then the candle. Concentrate for about a half hour on harmony, love and understanding being in the home, rather than friction, confusion and disappointment.

3. The next day use a bit of the Helping Hand incense as you meditate over the candle. Alternate the two incenses each day until you have brought and restored peace and good will back to the home.

4. If a large novena candle in glass is used, let it burn all the way. If a jumbo size candle is used, put it out after each day's meditation and continue until it is gone.

RETURN EVIL TO SENDERS

1. If you know for certain who has placed a spell upon you and you wish to return the favor, draw a figure of the person on a piece of parchment paper in Dragon's Blood ink or ritual black ink.

2. Write their name(s) on it and when the ink is dry, rub the paper with a mixture of Angelica and Agrimony herbs and Camphor Gum.

3. Each day you will light some Elemental incense and tear off a piece of the paper doll and burn it in the incense as you say:

Arise O Domballah!
O Victim you are seized, you are seized,
You are changed, flour hands become stilled,
you legs bend, your back hunches, your neck twists,
you teeth fall out and your loins fester.
O Victim release your sufferer or you the martyr will be!

In 5-15 days the person will have moved, disappeared or left you alone.

Caution: Karmic damage may occur as a result of using this spell.

CONTROL YOUR PROBLEMS

1 red bag	*1 tsp. Chickweed*
Controlling oil	*1 tsp. Ash leaves*
1 tsp. Basil	*1 tsp. Mugwort*
1 tsp. Rose petals	*1 Lodestone*
1 tsp. Lavender	*1 piece of parchment paper*
1 tsp. Bay leaves	

To control difficult problems in your life,
follow these directions carefully.

1. Using a red ink pen, write on the parchment paper the problem you wish to control. For example, if you need to win a court case, rent a house want a pay raise or whatever the problem. Then write the word "CONTROL" 3 times at the bottom.

2. Place a drop of Controlling oil on each corner of the paper and fold it 3 times and place it into the red bag.

3. Take the lodestone and put 3 drops of Controlling oil on it and place it in the bag. Then fill the bag with the herbs listed above.

4. Now say the following prayer:

OH, LORD, MAKE ME STOUT OF HEART,
GIVE ME THE POWER TO OVERCOME,
DRIVE THE EVIL FROM ME,
GIVE ME VICTORY, NEVER DESERT ME!

5. Close up the bag and carry it with you at all times and do not let anyone see it.

(continued)

6. At the same time every day, repeat the prayer and anoint the bag with the Controlling oil until you have controlled the problem.

Keep your faith strong! With a positive attitude and help from God, you will conquer your problem!

SEAL OF PROTECTION

The proper use of this seal will protect you from the evil influences of any person or spirit.

1. Draw this seal on a sheet of parchment paper using Dove's Blood Ink. On the reverse side, write your full name and birthdate.

2. Hold the seal pressed between the palms of both hands (in a *"praying hands"* position) and contemplate deeply on your desire to be protected.

3. Anoint the seal with Protection oil and place in a small red flannel sack. Carry the bag with you at all times. Anoint periodically with Protection oil whenever you feel the need. Do not allow anyone else to touch or see the bag.

Chapter 8
FINDING THE RIGHT
SPIRITUAL PRACTITIONER

I – RELIGION AND THE SPIRITUAL PRACTITIONER

FROM WHICH RELIGIOUS TRADITION SHOULD I CHOOSE MY PRACTITIONER?
With a very few exceptions, I don't believe in those practitioners who
claim to be "neutral" or "non-denominational." I do believe, however,
that certain practitioners can successfully operate outside of their own
religious traditions. To understand how this is possible, let us take a look
at some of the different religions. [13] Very broadly speaking, religions can
be divided into two great camps: Indigenous religions, often called "Native"
religions or "Primal," and historical religions, often called "Religions of
the Book." Some religions, like Hinduism, fall somewhere in the middle,
while others, like Palo, may not be religions at all, but magico-religious
systems. This brings us to the problematic of who decides what is a religion,
but that's a whole other can of worms!

Although the Roman Catholic Church has a great deal in common
with ceremonial magic with its appreciation for the power of rituals, it,
like most Religions of the Book, has been de-emphasizing its magical
components. The mass is no longer said in Latin, for example, and the
priest now looks at the audience rather than towards the image of God
while performing the Eucharistic rite. Lately, however, a new emphasis
on resurrecting the rite of exorcism among many Catholic dioceses in big
cities has been noted. My friend, the Melkite priest I mentioned earlier, is

one of several priests in the diocese of New York City authorized by the Roman Catholic Church to perform exorcisms [14] Other than the High Churches, such as the Catholics, Anglicans, and Eastern Orthodox, I find that Christian churches by and large do not emphasize belief in, or treatment of, psychic maladies. Evangelical Christians do not even treat those who do not convert to their beliefs.

I recommend a spiritual practitioner who, while dedicated to his religious beliefs, does not ask that his clients subscribe to them. For this reason, I believe spiritual practitioners with links to primal religions are the best. These include Afro-Diasporic priests and priestesses (Santeria, Candomble, Umbanda), Native American medicine men/women and Latin American shamans, Asian shamans, and all other indigenous practitioners who understand that the gift they have been given is to be universally distributed, regardless of the client's belief system.

IS A PRACTITIONER WITH ROOTS IN A PRIMAL RELIGION BETTER?

There are excellent spiritual advisors in all religions, in fact, I would think that the person being sought when one is experiencing spiritual difficulties should be one's own priest, rabbi, imam, or reverend. In reality, however, this doesn't always work out well. For example, take the case of an older Jewish woman who came to see me after her husband of 63 years died. "I don't want you to change my religion, Mr. Laremy," the woman said, "but I need you to do something for me my rabbi won't do." The woman went on to say that her husband had died unexpectedly and she had many unresolved issues she needed to discuss with him, but her rabbi told her that there was no way for her to communicate with her husband now. "In fact, he said he didn't even know if my husband was anywhere except six feet under." The woman then became agitated as she said, "After 63 years with this man, I need to know that his soul is not dead, Mr. Laremy, tell me he's not just six feet under! Please, tell me that he's not just six feet under!"' Since a great part of my practice consists in contacting dead relatives, it was easy for me to contact the spirit of the recently deceased man and allow his widow to seek closure in many issues that had remained unresolved between them. "I am not going to tell my rabbi I come to see you, Mr. Laremy, because he doesn't need to know," the woman said. "I appreciate you respecting my wish to retain my religion, but from time to time I'll need to contact my husband, and I'll come to you for that, if that's OK with you." The woman has remained a satisfied client for nearly two decades. I have numerous clients that are in similar positions. These are people who are mostly satisfied in their places of worship, but find that their religious leaders are not equipped to handle such situations as psychic attacks and those brought about by energy vampires. Many mainstream religions also refuse to contact or deal at all with the dead. These people require a great deal of discretion. Among the clients I have who fall into this category are rabbis, Christian clergymen, prominent politicians, and famous entertainers.

Those of us rooted in Primal religions belong to a paradigm that does not see a difference between life, magic, and religion; it is all part of the continuum of existence! We also know that the religion we practice may be the best suited for ourselves, but it may not be suited for the client who comes for help. Even though we may derive our power from our strong religiosity, we do not need to impose that religiosity on those who would benefit from our help. Like any other professional caregiver, the spiritual practitioner deserves remuneration for his or her services, and that is all he or she should expect from the client, not the client's conversion to the practitioner's religion! Unfortunately, Christian Evangelicals, Hare Krishnas, and many others, will perform a service such as an exorcism, ostensibly for free, but with the ulterior motive of converting the person in need. I have noticed that exorcisms done by such people are shoddy and, at best, temporary. The professional, serious, practitioner will integrate, as much as possible, the client's religion into the treatment, thus strengthening the client's own faith, rather than changing it.

II - NON-RELIGIOUS PRACTITIONERS

These fall mainly into three broad groups: Gypsies and their imitators, ceremonial magicians, including Paleros, Macumbeiros, etc., and "New Age" quacks. Gurus are a whole different bag of beans and I've given them a section of their own.

BEWARE OF THE GYPSIES. It leaves a bad taste in my mouth to have to talk negatively about a whole race, but, unfortunately, in the case of Gypsies, much of the bad stuff you've heard is true. When I was in college studying Theology, my roommate did his thesis on the Romany people, as Gypsies call themselves. I avidly helped him collect data and was excited by his initial proposal: that what was said about Gypsies was based on prejudice and discrimination and not true. After months of research we found that my friend's initial hypothesis was wrong. In brief, this is what he found:

Gypsies are a nomadic people originating in what is today northern India. During the middle ages, they arrived in Europe passing themselves off as Egyptian Christians running away from Moslem invaders, thus the name "Gypsy," a variation of "Egyptian." Here we see a pattern of deceit that they have raised to an art form, for, of course, they were neither Christian nor Egyptian. The name they call themselves is "Rom" or "Romany," apparently deriving from the Sanskrit "Ram," one of the names of God. Gypsies do not think that fooling the "gadjos," as they call the non-Gypsies, is bad. In fact, their religious myth gives them the right to steal because, they claim, a Gypsy stole the fourth nail that was to be put through Jesus, the one that was destined to cross his heart. For this reason, Jesus told that particular Gypsy that from that day on Gypsies would be allowed to steal from gadjos forevermore. Sadly, most gypsy fortune tellers are professional scam artists.[15] At least one Gypsy practitioner is trying to establish a bona-fide, honest, line. His name is Patrick Jasper Lee, and he is from England. He calls himself a "chovihano," which he says translates as "shaman."[16] For the most part, however, stay away from Gypsy practitioners, for a preponderance of evidence indicates they are more likely than not to be charlatans.

THE NON-RELIGIOUS PRACTITIONER. As far as I can tell, the only bona fide non-religious spiritual practitioner is the ceremonial magician or one of his counterparts. Ceremonial magic, Palo, sorcery, and Macumba all have similar aims; the manipulation of natural events through the use of magical control over supernatural forces by way of very specific rituals and ceremonies that, for whatever reasons, work. A ceremonial magician may not care about his/her relationship with God or his/her ethical obligations to his/her fellow sentient beings. Ceremonial magic is also unconcerned with community rituals or the betterment of mankind. Mainly because of these peculiarities, ceremonial magic falls short of what theologians, sociologists, and anthropologists have defined as "religion." Many ceremonial magicians are experts at interacting with what they refer to as archetypal forces, which may be labeled gods and demons. Expert ceremonial magicians can help clients with their problems, but most prefer not to work with clients, but to develop a close circle of like-minded individuals, all sworn to secrecy, that share their love of ceremonial magic and initiatic experiences. Anyone interested in ceremonial magic should seek a teacher/initiator. To practice ceremonial magic solely based on books is extremely dangerous. The following procedure speeds up the process of meeting the person who will be your teacher. Since ceremonial magic is utilitarian and not concerned with the means, as long as the desired end is reached, even people who do not believe in the Bible can obtain results by following these instructions.

STEP 1   Look for Psalm 95 in the Bible, put a bookmark on it so you don't lose your place.

STEP 2   Light purple candle (any size), and hold an amethyst in your left hand while you read psalm.

STEP 3   After reading Psalm, go to sleep with the amethyst under your pillow. You should dream the face of your teacher within six days.

NOTE: An added benefit of this practice is that, if you do it on a regular basis, it increases your clairvoyance.

PROTECTION AGAINST DEMONS. Because ceremonial magicians work a lot with demons, anyone contemplating that path should always Carry both the 101 st and 68th Psalm in a red flannel bag to ward off undesired demons!

Ceremonial magicians attain their power, which they call their *sanctum regnum* or "holy domain," through the development of four indispensable conditions, which the great 19th century magus, Eliphas Levy, described as follows:

> *"an intelligence illuminated by study, an intrepidity which nothing can check, a will which nothing can break, and a discretion which nothing can corrupt and nothing intoxicate. TO KNOW, TO DARE, TO WILL, TO KEEP SILENCE--such are the four words of the magus."* [17]

III- GURUVADA: THE WAY OF THE GURU

SHOULD I SEEK A "GURU?" When speaking of spiritual practices, no word is more charged with conflicting emotions than the word "guru," which was first popularized in America during the last part of the 19th century by an Indian Swami named Vivekananda, whose brilliance stunned visitors to Chicago's World's Fair nearly one hundred years ago. At first glance, the concept of guru appears to be in direct contradiction to many tenets Americans are taught to hold dear, so it is suprising to find that millions of Americans surrender their lives to gurus. In the 1960s a wave of interest in gurus, as well as everything Indian, was sparked by super-popular rock groups the Rolling Stones and the Beatles when they made very public trips to India to the ashram of an Indian holy man. The Beatles, for a time, publically declared their allegiance to Guru Maharishi Mahesh Yogi, who popularized a form of meditation called Transcendental Meditation, or TM for short. Other traditions have figures analogous to the Indian guru. These include the Oba of certain Yoruba-derived Afro-Diasporic sects, the "Padrino" or "Madrina" of some Santeria and Palo houses, and the Lamas of some forms of Buddhism.

Simply put, the guru represents the disciple's way to God. He (or she) is the finger that points to the Divine, and, according to guruvada (the way of the guru), you cannot understand God unless you meet a guru destined to explain him to you. In exchange for what the guru does for you, you have to surrender your heart and soul to the guru. The opportunity for abuse is obviously tremendous. It is said that the person who poses as a guru in order to take advantage of others receives punishment worse than ten thousand hells. On the other hand, finding one's true guru gives one constant protection from psychic attacks, initiation into the higher mysteries of life, a lifetime of learning the wonders of the universe, and the peace that comes from knowing that one has found God. To the disciple, there is no difference between the guru and God. A sign that you have met your guru is if you dream of him. Especially if you have a positive dream about him shortly after having met him or her. There is an old Indian saying that when you are ready to be taught, the teacher comes to you. So if you feel that the way of the guru is for you, be patient. Do not rush things. Keep yourself spiritually clean using the techniques I give you here so that it will be easier for your teacher to sense your vibrations and reveal him or herself to you.

Chapter 9
FINAL RECOMMENDATIONS

I - PRE-EMPTIVE ACTIONS

LIVING A LIFE NOT COMPATIBLE WITH NEGATIVITY. Negative energy, whether it comes from practitioners of evil, psychic vampires, non-human agents, or any other source, finds a rich feeding ground in a psyche weakened by lack of faith and corrupted by vice and violence. Find a spiritual practice that is compatible with your character and then stick with it, even if in the beginning it may seem boring to you. Maintain your home and your person clean and wellgroomed, believe it or not, negativity seems to attach itself to dirty, unkempt areas. Cultivate an aura of positivity and good cheer around you, be a "can-do" person rather than a "Can't do" one. If you can do someone a favor without hurting yourself, do so, by all means! and don't always expect to be reciprocated by that person, the favor you do for someone will eventually come back to you, but, most probably, not from that person, but from a totally unexpected source. Such are the ways of the Lords of Karma.

II - AN OUNCE OF PREVENTION

STUDY THIS BOOK CAREFULLY. Read this entire book from cover to cover with a yellow marker and a red marker on hand. If you are being actively attacked now, you need to address those concerns first. Mark in red all the treatments and remedies listed that may be of immediate help. Then carefully go over the pre-emptive treatments you and your family can make to keep the attacks from recurring. Mark these remedies in yellow, and make it a priority not to slack off, but to be strong. Surround yourself with positive people. Avoid those who drain you and bring you down. Even if such people are unavoidable, such as bosses, minimize your contact with them. Visualize an impenetrable bubble surrounding you when you are in their presence, and think to yourself, "I am strong, I am protected, there is nothing you can possibly do to me, because I am surrounded by the power of Love." There are plenty of amulets, prayers, and other techniques offered in this book to keep you safe until you discover your spiritual path.

III - FOLLOWING THE PATH

WALKING THE WALK AND TALKING THE TALK. After thirty-eight years of practice there is one generalization I can make about those I've helped. If they didn't already have one when they came to me, eventually, they all seek a spiritual path and either a close and trusting relationship with a spiritual advisor, or they enter into a learning path that makes them spiritual advisors themselves! Very few people are content to remain cold, aloof clients after witnessing the miracle of the Spirit. This doesn't mean that people join me or my religion, on the contrary, in my religion, which I am purposely not mentioning by name, we do not encourage converts. We believe that the roads that lead to God are as varied as human temperaments, and that which is right for me may be totally wrong for you. There are some religions that, by their very natures, present problems for the spiritual practitioners. I've had to turn down several Jehovah's Witnesses and Pentecostal Christians who came to me for help. These denominations specifically consider the work I do to be of a demonic character. These faiths believ. that if one doesn't accept Jesus as sole Savior of the entire universe, one is condemned to either a) annihilation *(Jehovah's Witnesses)* or b) eternal damnation in a fiery hell (Pentecostals). Some members of these denominations have sought my help out of their own desperation, but preliminary interviews with them revealed to me that, in their hearts, they still believed what their churches taught them. In other words, each one thought that going to a practitioner was wrong, but they would do it just because they were under such relentless attack. I do not accept such people, for in the long run, even if they do receive help from whatever attacks are undermining their faiths, feelings of guilt about having been seen by what they consider a "witch doctor" will cause more injury to their psyches than the demons I'd just dispelled from them. My advise to such people is to search within their churches for someone who can help them.

Although I try to remain neutral when it comes to denominations, I will admit to having a bias against those churches that say "if you don't believe in what I say you're going to hell." That intelligent, loving people can believe such crap is beyond my comprehension. Let's face it, I couldn't stand to see any of my children suffering even for a second, so how can God, who is so much more compassionate than I, stand still while billions of his children burn in the eternal flames of hell? Christians don't have a monopoly on short-sightedness., either. Nichiren Buddhists, including the aggressive proselytizers known as Sokka Gakkai, believe theirs is the only way. Some Muslims are also very radical. Even the Hare Krishna sect of notoriously open-minded Hinduism can fall prey to chauvinism, though admittedly the mildest of the three I just mentioned.

I believe there is transcendental beauty in the voyage a soul undertakes as it navigates through a sea of potentialities towards the blessed assuredness of that Terra Firma called TRUTH. Any spiritual practitioner worth his or her salt has to take a stand condemning any philosophy that would stifle such a wondrous trek. But such condemnation mustn't take the form of vitriolic attacks or unkind posturings. The condemnation acceptable to a spiritual person must be one clothed with compassion and right living, letting our example and unselfish nature be the healing heat that melts the ice of intransigence and pharisaic religiosity that often covers a warm and loving heart.

FOOTNOTES

1   Dion Fortune, *Psychic Self Defense* (London: Aquarian Press, 1959 [reprint of the 1930 edition])

2   If where you live there are no botanicas you can order from Original Publications by calling toll free (888) 622-8581 or (516) 454 6809.

3   You can also order Florida Water from Original (see preceding footnote).

4   If you believe you may possess evil eyes, the only way to obtain liberation from this unfortunate condition is to seek a spiritual practitioner who will guide you through the arduous process of changing your nature.

5   Or her, of course.

6   I have not attempted to correct the apparently awkward and stilted writing style of the prayer, as it has worked this way for hundreds of years. R.L.

7   Aleister Crowley (1875-1947), the greatest ceremonial magician of the 20th century, began the practice of adding a letter k to the word "magic" in order to distinguish it from the stage illusionist's kind.

8   Not all macumbeiros and mayomberos work evil.

9   Each time this symbol appears, make the sign of the cross over the water.

10   Some practitioners add "for thine is the kingdom, and the power, and the glory, now and always and forever and ever, Amen," but by tradition only priests are allowed to say the entire prayer.

11   Dorothy Morrison, *Everyday Magic* (St. Paul: Llewellyn, 2000), p.247.

12   Contrary to what many people from the U.S. believe, they are not the only Americans. Anyone from North, Central, and South American can call him/herself AMERICAN also.

13   Since I hold a masters in Religious Studies and have served as expert witness in many courts of law, I speak with some authority on this subject.

14   'The Melkite rite, while allowing its priests to be married, is still under the jurisdiction of the pope and is considered part of the Byzantine rite of the Roman Catholic Church.

15   For more information, read Peter Maas's book *King of the Gypsies*.

16   Read about Patrick Jasper Lee in *Shaman's Drum* No. 51, Spring 1999, Pp. 30-39.

17   Eliphas Levy, *The Doctrine and Ritual of Magic*, n.d.

BIBLIOGRAPHY

Canizares, Raul. *Cuban Santeria,* Destiny Books, Rochester, Vt. 2000.

Cavendish, Richard. *The Black Arts,* Routledge, London, 1967.

Fortune, Dion *Psychic Self-Defence,* Aquarian Press, London, 1959 (reprint of 1930 edn.).

Gamache, Henri. *The Master Book of Candle Burning* Original Publications: Plainview, NY, 1998.

Levi, Eliphas *Transcendental Magic, its Doctrine and Rituals* Dutton, NY n.d.

Mickaharic, Draja. *Spiritual Cleansings,* Samuel Weiser Inc., York Beach, ME, 1982.

Morrison, Dorothy. *Everyday Magic,* Llewellyn, St. Paul, 2000.

Skaff, Archimandrite Elias B. *My Faithful Guide to the Byzantine Melkite Liturgy,* Brooklyn, N. Y. ,1975

ITEM #216
$9.95

HELPING YOURSELF WITH SELECTED PRAYERS
-VOLUME 2-
OVER 170 PRAYERS!

The prayers from Volume 2 come from diverse sources. Most originated in Roman Catholicism and can still be found in one form or another on the reverse of little pocket pictures of saints, or in collections of popular prayers. Another source for these prayers is the French Spiritist movement begun in the 1800's by Allan Kardec, which has become a force in Latin America under the name Espiritismo. The third source, representing perhaps the most mystical, magical, and practical aspects of these prayers, is found among the indigenous populations where Santería has taken root.

These prayers will provide a foundation upon which you can build your faith and beliefs. It is through this faith that your prayers will be fulfilled. The devotions within these pages will help you pray consciously, vigorously, sincerely and honestly. True prayer can only come from within yourself.

Item #222
$11.95

THE PSALM WORKBOOK
by Robert Laremy
Work with the Psalms to
Empower, Enrich and Enhance Your Life!

This LARGE PRINT King James version of the Book of Psalms contains nearly 400 simple rituals and procedures that can be used to help you accomplish anything you desire. Use the situational index provided to decide which psalm to pray for your specific need.

Peace, Protection, Health,
Success, Money, Love,
Faith, Inspiration, Spiritual Strength
And much more!

Approach your worship with a clean heart and a child-like faith in God's infinite wisdom and you will derive tremendous results from the powers of the psalms.

ITEM #172
$9.95

HELPING YOURSELF WITH
MAGICKAL OILS A-Z
BY MARIA SOLOMON

The most thorough and comprehensive workbook available on the

Magickal Powers of Over 1000 Oils!

Easy to follow step-by-step instructions
for more than 1500
Spells, Recipes and Rituals for
Love, Money, Luck, Protection
and much more!

ISBN 0-942272-49-8 5½"x 8½" $9.95

ITEM #224
$6.95

Revised and Expanded

Success and Power Through Psalms

By Donna Rose

For thousands of years, men and women have found in the Psalms the perfect prayer book, possessing wisdom applicable to every human situation. Wise men and women of deep mystical insight have also learned to decipher the magical formulas David and the other Psalmists hid behind the written words. These formulas help the seeker solve everyday problems, achieve higher states of consciousness, gain material and spiritual wealth, as well as help defend himself or herself against psychic attacks and all manner of dangers.

The Revised and Expanded edition of Donna Rose's classic offers over 300 simple to perform magical rituals to help you manifest all of your desires using the magical powers of the psalms.

ISBN 0-942272-79-X 5½"x 8½ $6.95

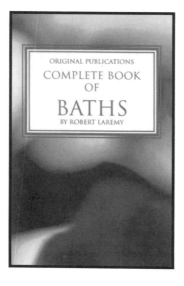

ORIGINAL PUBLICATIONS
COMPLETE BOOK
OF
BATHS
BY ROBERT LAREMY

ITEM #592
$8.95

COMPLETE
BOOK OF BATHS

By Robert Laremy

Featuring recipes for :

*Love, Money, Health, Happiness, Spiritual Growth,
Psychic Defense, Fighting Bad Habits and much more!*

It is important when taking a spiritual bath to understand that it is different from a regular bath. A normal bath is a necessary sanitary function that removes the dirt and grime of daily living, a spiritual or ritual bath has a totally different aim: to remove unwanted energies and baleful vibrations. The act of undertaking a spiritual bath indicates that the person doing it is a believer in the higher truths. This belief in itself triggers the necessary energies that, mixed with the physical attributes of the ingredients chosen, facilitates the elimination of the unwanted vibrations and the acquisition of positive energies.

ISBN 0-942272-73-0 5½"x 8½" $8.95

TOLL FREE: 1 (888) OCCULT - 1

ITEM #053
$8.95

PAPA JIM'S
HERBAL MAGIC
WORKBOOK

Papa Jim is a very famous healer and root doctor. He brings you this compilation of remedies and potions from all over the world. Share the secret recipes that have mystically solved the problems of Papa Jim's many devotees. Learn how to unleash the magical powers of herbs.

Follow easy instructions on how to make
Herbal Baths, Mojo Bags, Sprinkling Powders,
Incenses and Teas for Love, Luck, Sex,
Money Drawing, Gambling
Protection, Hex Breaking, Jinx Removing and more!

Also incudes
English to Spanish / Spanish to English
translation for over 150 common herbs!

ISBN 0-942272-64-1 5½"x 8½" 112 pages $8.95

ITEM #065
$6.95

Unhexing and Jinx Removing

By Donna Rose

Everywhere we turn these days it seems as if there are forces working against us. You don't need to spend your time thinking, worrying about or stressing over the evils that are constantly prowling. Cast out all forces of negativity, evil thoughts, evil intentions, evil spirits and so on. Break up conspiracies, dispel rumors, blanket your enemies with suffering and confusion. Believe it or not there are ways to protect yourself in this modern world. The easy to perform rituals and spells provided in this book will allow you to escape the dangers hounding you.

ISBN 0-942272-84-6 5½"x 8½" $6.95

TOLL FREE: 1 (888) OCCULT - 1   WWW.OCCULT1.COM

New Revised
The
Master
Book
of
Candle
Burning

How to Burn
Candles
for Every Purpose

POWERFUL
PSALM
RITUALS

HENRI
GAMACHE

Item# 043
$9.95

"How can I burn candles in a manner which will bring me the most satisfaction and consolation?"

In order to answer that question it is necessary to eliminate all technical, dry and often times torturous historical background. It is necessary to sift and sort every fact, scrutinize every detail, search for the kernel.

It is to be hoped that this volume answers that question in a manner which is satisfactory to the reader. It has been necessary, of course, to include some historical data and other anthropological data in order to better illustrate the symbolism involved in modern candle burning as practiced by so many people today.

This data has been accumulated from many sources: it has been culled from literally hundreds of books and articles. The modern rituals outlined here are based upon practices which have been described by mediums, spiritual advisors, evangelists, religious interpreters and others who should be in a position to know.

It has been the author's desire to interpret and explain the basic symbolism involved in a few typical exercises so that the reader may recognize this symbolism and proceed to develop his own symbolism in accordance with the great beauty and highest ethics of the Art.

ISBN 0-942272-56-0 5½"x 8½" $9.95